YOU ASK YOURSELF

Is this my fault?
What if he refuses my help?
Should I continue to bail her out of trouble?
Can we save our marriage?
Should I threaten to leave?
Will he come home drunk again?
Will she come home at all?

If you are a co-dependent partner of an alcoholic you've probably asked yourself these questions a thousand times. But you are not alone. Now Jack Mumey offers you the help and hope you need to make it—one day at a time.

LOVING AN ALCOHOLIC

Help and Hope for Significant Others

Jack Mumey

BANTAM BOOKS
TORONTO · NEW YORK · LONDON · SYDNEY · AUCKLAND

For my partner, Paul

"... I have a partner, Mr. Jorkins. ... Mr. Jorkins has his opinions on these subjects, and I am bound to respect Mr. Jorkin's opinions. ..."

CHARLES DICKENS, *David Copperfield*

Contents

Part IV—THE BRIGHT FUTURE

Preface

With the writing of this book, I complete a trilogy on alcoholism that was started four years ago. In whatever way I have been able to contribute, my readers have been given an opportunity to change their lives, lives that have been altered forever by the appearance of alcoholism in their midst.

The Joy of Being Sober was written for recovering alcoholics, people like me, discovering that living a life free from alcohol is the most rewarding and fulfilling existence they could ever hope for! *Joy* is also a book for those who love recovering alcoholics, but it is intended more to promote understanding than to serve as the working manual that this volume is.

In *Sitting in the Bay Window*, the particular problems facing parents of alcoholics, particularly young ones, were addressed, and some new tools were offered to help such parents face and deal with the perplexing agonies that are uniquely theirs.

Now we look at another very special set of people. We call them *co-dependents*, *co-alcoholics* or *significant others*, the term under which I have come to know and love so many of them. At Gateway Treatment Center, founded and operated by my partner Paul F. Staley and me, hundreds of significant others have come through the doors.

Most get well along with their alcoholics. Many fall by the wayside and continue to lead unproductive and sick lives, refusing to make the changes and take the risks that are necessary to free themselves from the alcoholic chains that have kept them bound for so much of their lives.

Either way, you can't help feeling a special love and concern for these dogged souls who bravely work at "keeping up a good front" while they slowly and firmly die inside, unable to face and deal with the problems of living with and *loving* a person afflicted with the disease of alcoholism.

This book is, like my others, a tool. Like all other tools, it must be picked up and used to get any benefit from it at all. It is certainly not the *total* answer, as no tool alone does the complete job, but rather takes its proper place in the whole project.

It is my hope that *Loving an Alcoholic* will find its rightful place among the arsenals of treatment for these special people, the significant others, and will be used by them as a guide to where they have come from, what they may do to change, and how their future can be brighter and more fulfilling than ever.

To help me accomplish such a goal, many people have given me support as both an author and a therapist, not to mention lifelong support in my recovery as a sober alcoholic.

The dedication of this book, to my partner Paul Staley, is a small token of the esteem and friendship for Paul that has grown over the years that we have been associated. In every chapter of this book, I assure you, there is the fine-honed influence of my work with Paul. I thank him for that, for it is a gift that cannot be otherwise purchased.

With equal dedication, my editor, Shari Lesser, has guided and fine-tuned every step of the development of this book, as well as the direction of the first two volumes, and I hope whatever work from me that will cross her desk in the future.

My life as an author, open to the public and its praises and criticisms, and as a private person, seeking refinement of this business of living, has changed considerably over the last few years. People often ask for more personal disclosure from me than is always therapeutically good or particularly necessary for successful treatment. On the other hand, it stands to reason that you have a natural curiosity about the author whose works you take into your homes and into your lives, for however short a period of time. Therefore, I proffer an update to satisfy the curious, to bond the reader to the writer.

New faces have crossed the horizons to join others who have had particular influence on my development as a writer and a person. Each is important in his or her own way.

My older daughter, Tracey, is a successful lawyer, fulfilling her and my struggles together to find the ways to make it happen. So many times it appeared we would not be able to pull it off, but we counted on our love to work its special magic of father for daughter.

My son, Jackson, is the proudest "drum-beater" for his dad that any man could want, all the while continuing to build his own successful real estate management career and a wonderful family at the same time. He is a constant source of pride, independence, and fellowship for me.

You've got to have twins to know how special they are, and I am blessed to have these two different, yet so alike, beautiful young ladies. They make their dad alternately proud and frustrated that he has been unable to read their particular mood or intent in some action taken or forgotten.

Twin daughter Dana is following Tracey into the halls and mysteries of the law, working on her degree with the fervor and singleness of purpose that makes her the special person she is, loving and earnest.

Twin daughter Dawn has chosen to follow me into the field of therapy, working with families and individuals with a very special skill that she possesses and uses with love, care, and concern. She, too, is gifted, exasperating, and fun!

Each of these four children—nay, young adults—has contributed time, patience, nagging, frustration, support, and, mostly, love, as I have struggled to put my thoughts into my Epson QX-10 computer. "Eppie" and I could never have made it without their support, and I thank them for it and hope they know of my deep, abiding love for them all.

Even though our lives have taken us in different directions, Mary Jo Mumey has remained a close friend, staunch supporter, and fond contributor to my writing.

Pastor Del Wiemers and Pastor Dave Peters are the kind of men that have always found the time to make me feel welcome. Del never has given up on me, even when there was every reason to do so! My friends Ron and Anada Gusé provide the kind of haven a writer needs; they never ask anything in return for giving me the sanctuary I sometimes need, and I am grateful to them.

"Laney" has been there for me when it has been important.

Her sons, Matt, Ken, and Don, I am proud to call my friends.

Finally, to all the significant others who have sat so uncomfortably in the same room with me as I sometimes unmercifully confronted them about what they wanted to do to make their lives better, I say a profound "thank you." Your unflagging energy has made it possible for you to keep working on getting better, to be willing to change, to find some new avenue of approach to learning how to live with and love the alcoholic with whom you have been involved through both the active and sober states of the disease. Without you, this book would not have been possible, and it really belongs to you, for whatever help it will be now and in the future.

> *But O the heavy change, now thou art gone,*
> *Now thou art gone and never must return!*

> JOHN MILTON, *Lycidas 1*

Part I

THE SEVEN DEADLY
SINS OF THE PAST

1

Your Shame

"My God! How could *this* happen to me?"

"What'll Mom and Dad think?"

"How can I *ever* face my friends again? I'm *so* embarrassed!"

Shame. *Your* shame. Born from the seemingly endless nights spent with your alcoholic, whose behavior was absolutely devasting to you. The long, haggard mornings that found you sitting by the telephone, hesitant to make the calls that you felt compelled to make:

"Trish, I'm calling to say I'm sorry for the way things got out of hand last night. Brad must've been very tired from work. He doesn't usually let his drinks get to him like that!"

"Mom? I . . . I . . . hardly know what to say! Honestly! I've just never heard Brad talk like that! The first thing this morning he wanted me to call and apologize!"

So there you are, running the playlet through the theater of your mind, triggering a massive feeling of shame, shame that you could have become involved with an alcoholic.

For a long time you have been trying to kid yourself into thinking that the person you love and want to respect might just have a "little drinking problem." But, as the days, weeks, months, and perhaps years roll by, the painfully obvious becomes crystal clear. You *are* involved with an alcoholic.

It seems as if your shame grows by leaps and bounds,

3

making you feel as if you need to go about with either a sack over your head or a large sign warning others to stay away.

These feelings are very natural, as you will soon discover as we journey together through the pages of this book. What is helpful, I think, is to break down the major areas of the "shame syndrome" as I have observed it from working with dozens of our own significant-other patients at our Gateway Treatment Center.

Parents and Other Family Members

It is natural to want to please our parents or other family members that have been very close to us. Grandmothers who raised us, grandfathers who nurtured us in the place of absent or deceased fathers, favorite uncles and aunts who all tended to influence our behaviors, and thus leave their marks on our lives, have a vested interest in us.

We learn to make many of the major decisions of our lives with both some conscious and unconscious consideration of "How will Mom and Dad (or others) feel about this?"

In spite of all our claims to independent living, "no man is an island," as John Donne reminded us, and we seek and crave parental approval for our lives and our lifestyles. Therefore, something so monumental in our lives as hooking up with an alcoholic, whether by marriage or just close relationship, can provoke a devastating amount of shame.

The question is: How do you get rid of these feelings?

The answer is twofold: (1) by educating both yourself and those in your family for whom you have special concern and (2) by giving back the *power over another's life that you never had in the first place!*

If you can understand the disease of alcoholism and the fact that it has come to the person in your life through several ancestral lines or sources, then you can also understand that *you have no reason to apologize* to any mother, father, aunt, uncle, or whatever, for something into which you never had any input from the beginning.

We'll talk more about the disease itself as we go along, but for now it's enough for you to understand that a disease has very little or nothing to do with willpower, character, backbone, stick-to-it-iveness, or any other of those things that our parents instill in us as wholesome and desirable character traits. Therefore, you don't have to be shameful in front of your family because you are involved with a person who has that disease.

Part of the shame you may feel, however, is the shame that says, "I should have known better, Mom (or Dad)!" But really, now, how could you know? And even if you did know, would that really have deterred you from going on with the relationship? Probably not, unless you are a "two-time loser," and have firsthand knowledge of what life with a practicing alcoholic can be like.

When parents or other family members confront you about your alcoholic and, more importantly, about your "continuing to put up with it," and begin spouting off about the alcoholic's lack of backbone, character, and so on, you can break the old habits of your past that made you hang your head in shame by informing your family of the *disease*. This does not, of course, excuse the fact that neither you nor your alcoholic has done anything to treat this disease yet, but it does allow you to throw off the yoke of shame that you hand-selected this "failure" and thus brought shame upon your family.

In the past you have felt that you have let down your family, your friends, yourself. You have felt that you must constantly apologize for behaviors that are really not in your power to control!

That brings us to point two: Your shame in the past has been fed, nurtured, allowed to grow unchecked, because you honestly believed you had power over someone else's life! Doesn't that sound strange as you sit here reading this? Nobody that I know of gave you any such power; your God certainly didn't look down from on high and grant you any such power; the alcoholic in your life sure as hell never offered you any such power. So where, pray tell, did you get it?

You took it! You *created* it. You honestly led yourself to believe that you could control the alcoholic behavior of the person in your life who is contributing to such shame. It stands to reason, therefore, that you, believing you possessed such a power, needed to apologize for not exercising this power. Now admit it! That's what you've done in the past. When parents and other close relatives have confronted you about the behavior of "Brad" or "Kim," you felt the shame creeping up in you, the shame of your own inaction to put into motion all this power you thought you had.

Doesn't it make sense, therefore, to give up this power you never had in the first place and hence give up the shame that has gone with you every time Mom, Dad, Grandma, or Aunt Sue made your alcoholic a subject for conversation (which is generally 75 to 80 percent of the time)? Think about it!

Siblings

Your brothers and sisters may have always looked up to you in the past or do so now by virtue of all sorts of obvious family dynamics. On the other hand, they may have never looked up to you, and the fact that you are involved with an alcoholic (recovering or not) only cements their feelings that you could never do anything right.

So the shame of your past in relation with your siblings makes it difficult for you to talk to them about the situation in which you may find yourself. So what have you been doing? You have been defending, that's what! Every time a brother or sister confronts you about your "mistake" or your "putting up with it" life, you start throwing darts at them for all the mistakes *they* have made in life.

So you deal with your own shame by heaping some shame on them. And why not? It always worked in the past, when you were all growing up, so why shouldn't it work now? But that's no way to handle this false shame.

Your brothers and sisters will need patient education and understanding from you as you learn it yourself, and that's one of the strongest reasons we will constantly be stressing *family* treatment for alcoholism in this book.

This shame in relation to your siblings is different from that felt toward other family members because you have such a different and special relationship with each other. Your relationship with brothers and sisters has either bound you very close together in times of trouble or split you very far apart in terrible anger, jealousy, and downright hatred.

Shame, therefore, can become a powerful weapon in your siblings' hands, and you can be a most willing target as you have been in the past, allowing your shame to be the platform from which other brothers and sisters can launch a wide variety of attacks on you. In the past, you have taken it, particularly if you have considered yourself as the brother or sister that everyone else looked up to.

The fact that you could possibly now be failing their expectations of you continues to nurture your shame.

Close Friends

Here again, you have been something special in the eyes of your really close friends. These are fraternity brothers, sorority sisters, your best man and maid or matron of honor, the secret-keeping friend, the trusted colleague or golfing or tennis partner, as opposed to the casual acquaintances of your life.

The shame you have experienced with these people is born of your failure to act on the situation. You have probably found yourself actually apologizing for having done nothing about it. The fact that you may have tried to do something and failed is even more devastating when you are in the company of these special people in your life.

The endless queries over watercress sandwiches, a hand of bridge, a set of tennis, or a game or two of bowling have made you so edgy that your friends began to wonder what was really happening to you, the old friend they had always known and loved for strength of character, the action-oriented, problem-solving kind of guy or gal you've always appeared to be.

You may have retreated so far away from your intimate friendships that times normally spent enjoying each other's company are now spent in amateur therapy sessions, with your friend trying to get to the bottom of what's wrong with you. God help you if you refuse the friendly beer or glass of wine that you and your friend have always shared! "Do *you* have a problem, too?" becomes a new topic for conversation, and your shame has prevented you from dealing with things like this from any position of strength.

Co-Workers, Boss, Ex-Mates

This is another category that is unique when you are recalling the shame of your past. Your co-workers know that something is not quite right, sense that there is something wrong in your life, but they may not be close enough to you to fall into the category of confidants. So you have exhibited shame in being in the alcoholic relationship. You have answered questions about your past weekend with the kinds of answers that make you the hot topic at coffee breaks and lunches, where everyone conveniently shuts up when you join the group. These past actions have only enhanced the co-workers' feelings that you are terribly ashamed of whatever it is that's going on in your life.

You haven't done a whole lot better with your boss.

"Janie, you seem to be preoccupied. Anything you want to tell me?" inquires your boss.

"God, no!" you think, afraid even to hint that you have been going through an unspeakable and private hell. "I've just got a bad headache, Mister Thompson." So you have allowed your shame to isolate you from yet another person who might have been reaching out in sympathy, but for whom you have no desire to start the whole list of excuses that you have been using in the past. Ever present in your mind is the fear that, if your boss really knew, it might cost you your job; a career might go down the tubes; at the very least, a promotion would be jeopardized!

Ex-mates, whether ever actually married to you or not, pose a different catalyst that has fed into your shame pantry. Inquiries from these people about your continued involvement with "poor old Tom" and questions such as "Does Marney still hit the juice pretty hard?" have all tended to isolate you and increase the depth of your shame. These people from your intimate past seem to be standing on the corner of the busiest street of your life and pointing a great big accusatory finger at you for all to see.

"Lookee there, folks! She is making another big mistake! Got herself all tangled up with an alcoholic!"

It has been enough in the past to make you want to crawl away and hide, except there hasn't been a place large enough to hide you and your shame from this ex-mate's imagined (or real) taunting, whether imagined or real. Your shame has given power to these people to hurt you over and over again.

If the ex has had a problem with alcohol—if that was one of the reasons you split up—your shame has kept you burrowing even farther down in the ground of your own despair.

Casual Acquaintances

Casual acquaintances almost always have been a source of embarrassment for you. You have just met someone or have been to a gathering of some kind, and your alcoholic, if still actively drinking, has "acted out of line." Your shame has been of some great proportion, depending on how much you had counted on making and *keeping* new friends. In the past, you have probably gone to the friends who arranged the party or the ones who introduced you and your alcoholic to the new people and asked them to "explain" the behavior of the day or evening before.

Either way it came down, your shame played a significant role in helping you stay in the frame of mind that says, "I'm trapped!" So many times, the significant others like you have counted on breaking out of a particular circle of friends they falsely believe are all responsible for the amount of drinking that is being done by the alcoholic.

You have hoped that meeting new people would be that magic that you have been seeking, but now, once again, your shame has convinced you that it's just another replay of the same old tape. But the embarrassment of these casual acquaintances has flowed over and onto the parties that are your primary friends, and you have felt deeply ashamed for them and for you.

Potential New Friends

This is a slightly different category in your shame of the past. In this case, you have been avoiding introductions to new people who might have breathed some fresh air into your alcoholic existence. But you steadfastly refuse to accept invitations that might put you in a position that is potentially dangerous—dangerous in that you might just accept an invitation that will involve new people. You fear your alcoholic will display those old behaviors, and your shame will drive you out of this new circle. So you have allowed your past shame to say, "No, thank you. We have other plans."

What a tragedy! Yet this scenario is played out over and over, thousands of times, day and evening, all over the world by those significant-other persons, like you, who have allowed shame to be a controlling factor in their lives.

So, in our examination of the first of the seven deadly sins of your past, you hopefully have been painfully reminded of the manner in which you have felt shame, allowed shame to be a controlling factor, and made shame the reason for not dealing with your family, siblings, co-workers, intimate or casual friends.

Of course, the *real* victim has been you. This "Sin" of shame has been a real crippler! It has prevented you from truly facing your problem squarely and from taking any kind of action that would better your position in life and that of your alcoholic. But do you know what? You've become pretty *comfortable* with this shame!

We don't often associate a word like *comfortable* with a feeling like shame, but it has happened to you. Throughout this book I will be reminding you that considering making changes in your life is scary. It's downright frightening to take the kinds of risk involved in making change. You have, therefore, become comfortable with being sick!

A lot of you are probably offended by that statement, reacting just the way you can be expected to. Namely, it is the alcoholic that is sick, isn't it? What gives me the right to accuse *you* of being sick? But, like it or not, if you will at least be very honest with yourself, you will realize that the mere fact that you have done nothing or very little to change your circumstances tells you that you have become accustomed to your role and that your shame, along with the other seven deadly sins of your past, has allowed you to remain in an unhealthy or sick state.

You have been giving and receiving double messages. These are messages that say, on the one hand, "I'm in a predicament here and don't know what to do." The other part of the message says, "I'm comfortable with where I am, or at least I'm operating OK where I am, so why change?"

Your shame has kept you where you are, not moving forward and unable to face your family and friends with any sense of security about your situation, but only with excuses for the behaviors that everyone sees and recognizes as alcoholic in nature.

The problem with the double message stated above is that you are *not* OK where you are. You have just allowed your shame to make you think you are, and the risk has been too great for you to move out of the depths of your life and face the issue squarely. As we progress through Part I, we will lay out the remainder of the seven deadly sins of your past. As they come face up on the table before you, you will see an emerging pattern, one that shows you have been caught in a web of your own making and in the past have made no attempts to break free.

What makes us afraid to take risks? As Shakespeare

has the melancholy Dane, Hamlet, tell himself, "The undiscover'd country . . . makes us rather bear those ills we have than fly to others we know not of."

Your "undiscovered country" is the unknown, the fearful future that might speak clearly to you of separation or divorce from, or ultimately death of, the alcoholic in your life. Therefore, you have allowed yourself to stay stuck in neutral; at least you *know* what your life is like now.

Honestly, now, is that *really* what you want from life? I think not! So let us continue together to examine the other emotions—the "sins" of your past that have prevented you from the risk taking of your future.

2

Your Anger

You may have waited a long time for the serious relationship that you are in. When he or she came along, it certainly seemed to you that you had found the ideal companion; there was joy in your heart!

And then the other shoe dropped. Slowly, but steadily, the knowledge has crept up on you that you have involved yourself with someone who has "a drinking problem." That problem has grown to an almost agonized reality. The person you have anchored your "ship of dreams" to has more than a drinking problem; he or she is an alcoholic!

The devastation of such a discovery has given way to a Mount Vesuvius within your mind and your body. The volcano has exploded, and the lava of your frustration with your situation has run into a sea of anger that is controlling your life.

You have been snapping at everybody and everything. If people didn't know you better, they would believe it is *you* who is in trouble with alcohol because your temper has been so quick to flare of late.

"Don't ask Joannie anything this morning, Merv! She'll decapitate you right at your desk!"

"My God, Fred, why are you jumping down everyone's throat today? What did *we* do to deserve this?"

Well, you get the idea. You have been living like that from day to day, knowing you weren't being yourself, but not knowing what to do about it. In fact, you haven't even been able to put a real finger on the different kinds of anger that have permeated your otherwise jocular personality. Your anger has been buried—not talked about or acted on—and that anger, "stuffed" within you, has turned to deep, deep resentment.

I believe, however, that your anger has not been focused on just the alcoholic in your life. That would be too dangerous. It might mean sacrificing the relationship, and that is something you have been unable and reluctant to do. That very inaction is what has kept you locked into this relationship, unwilling and unable to do anything about it.

So, let's take a look at the five areas of anger that have served as the arenas in which you have been doing battle daily. One type of anger has, of course, been directed at the alcohol abuser, but your alcoholic probably has not received the brunt of your past anger. It simply has been a waste of your time and energy to try to talk sense to your alcoholic, so you have turned to some other sources that have provided ready grist for your anger mill. Please keep in mind that these are what I feel are the obvious objects of your anger; you probably can add to the list. You might freely substitute as well, but the point is to recognize that you have not been very productive lately, allowing this anger to get very much in the way of any progress *both* of you could make in getting well.

Anger at Self

You have not really wanted to address this particular anger in your past, and why should you? Perhaps you feel that you made a "mistake" by choosing this partner. Well, no one wants to admit having made a mistake, particularly in the choice of a mate or a companion. It always becomes more painfully clear when we see someone who waited until somewhat late in life to choose a companion and then discovers, the hard way, that the chosen mate is an alcoholic. It does little for the ego or for your confidence in making the really important decisions in your life.

So you have vented your frustrations on everyone except the person who greets you in the mirror every morning! You have also fallen into a trap of believing that it really wasn't your mistake after all. Maybe, you think, the whole thing has been a temporary problem, and when it goes away you won't have to be angry anymore. But it isn't going to just go away, and unless you can honestly face yourself and allow yourself to be angry at *you*, you will just be another inhabitant of the mythical Land of Oz!

Even if you haven't been willing to face it, anger at yourself has probably already manifested itself in a number of ways. You have not taken very good care of yourself, for example. You have probably put on a few pounds, eating your frustration and anger into deepseated resentments. Or you might have gone into a depressive weight loss, where the number of calories you put away just seem to roll off you, and you have found yourself slipping another notch over on your belt.

"That's great!" you may think. "That's what I want to do—*lose weight!*" But it's *not* great, because weight loss that occurs due to depression is *not* what is recommended or advised for a healthy you. Look at what you have been wearing: Have your clothes been as bright or vibrant? Have you been letting your inward anger make you just not give a damn how you looked?

When was the last time you had your hair styled? When did you care for your nails? When you selected your wardrobe in the morning, was it with excitement for what the day might bring, or was it just another old outfit?

This kind of noncaring about how you look has been your way of subconsciously punishing yourself for waiting for a special person in your life, who then turned out to be alcoholic. Anger at yourself can account for the fact that your shoes aren't shined, that your car is dirty and messy on the inside as well as out, that your body has begun to reflect your inward anger in many ways.

You have become careless of wearing a coat on days you know call for rainwear or snow protection. You almost flirt with the idea of catching whatever the current rage is; the Asian flu is courted by you as a means of paying yourself back for "being so stupid" as to fail to recognize your alcoholic as such.

The self-anger you surely have not dealt with is the anger that has immobilized you and kept you from doing anything positive about the alcoholic, such as treatment, A.A., individual help for yourself, etc. This is not even to mention the awful agonies that have prevented you from even considering separation or divorce. Even the thought of just *ending* the relationship has been a nightmare for you!

These are just some of the manifestations of your self-anger. There are dozens of other ways in which you seem to have punished yourself without realizing that some of your anger has been self-directed.

The crying jags that have been a part of your past; the way you have slammed in and out of your living quarters, as if you were trying to break some unseen chains that were keeping you in this hellish bondage day after day— these are just two of the behaviors that you may have been exhibiting over the days, weeks, or months during which anger at yourself has been building.

Anger at the Alcoholic

There is no question that the prime target of your anger has been the alcoholic. After all, if it weren't for the abuser, you wouldn't have been feeling this way, would you? But here the anger that you have felt is almost entirely on the surface; you have been powerless to do a whole lot about your loved one's drinking. In fact, I have found that conversations with an alcoholic about drinking quickly turn into sessions in which the alcoholic spends the majority of the time telling you what is wrong with you!

Hasn't that been the pattern in your past? Of course it has! We know this about you because we know that the alcoholic is very skillfull in being able to shift the focus away from his drinking and find something that's wrong with you! The alcoholic does this in order to get you focused on yourself and off the alcoholic's drinking. He will do *almost anything* to protect "the right" to drink.

So you have been angry at the alcoholic, but you've

not been able to convert that anger to much positive action. In fact, the anger has been buried so often and has festered into such deep resentment for the alcoholic that you can barely remember the good parts of your relationship.

It's been a very frustrating time of your life, and each new drinking episode only contributes to the frustration. You have seen things get progressively worse, both in the drinking and in the deterioration of the relationship.

Your anger has come spilling out with such statements as:

"If you *really* loved me, you'd quit!"

"Where's your *willpower*, for God's sake!"

"Can't you be a *man*, a *real man?*"

"Is *this* your idea of how a *real lady* acts?"

And so it goes. You supply your own dialogue; I can only assure you it won't be very original because it gets played out in the little theaters of alcoholic relationships all over the world, every day. The languages may be different, but the pain, anger, shame, and the rest of the seven deadly sins of your past are vented between people who are caught in the web of untreated alcoholism.

If the anger you have at the alcoholic *can't* be vented, and if you have *not* treated this anger in an appropriate manner, then you can count on the fact that other people have been the recipients of it.

Anger at Society

There is very little doubt that you have pretty much been angry at the whole world. The reason for your anger is seemingly logical: Why does society have to make such a big damn deal out of drinking, anyway?

You have come to resent seeing the many ads for alcoholic beverages in newspapers and magazines. You can hardly tolerate another beer commercial on television. You have become terribly aware of how many drinking scenes are played out in your favorite soap or in weekly episodes of whatever favorite program has become a part of your TV-watching habits.

To paraphrase the shouted outbursts from the movie

Network, you're mad as hell and not going to take it anymore! The problem with this anger is, of course, that you are powerless to change the world. The society in which we live is geared to such things. Drinking is a fact of American social life, and what you have failed to remember is that alcoholics represent a minority of people in our society.

Your anger at the people who can and do drink responsibly is understandable, but it is futile. It is *your* loved person who has the problem, and even though you have felt like there is too much drinking going on in our society, it is inappropriate to display anger toward the whole world of social drinkers.

When TV programs that you are watching reveal drunkenness on the part of certain characters, you have probably received a basketful of snide remarks from the alcoholic sitting beside you. This has made you all the more angry, but because your pattern has been not to deal with that anger, once again you have buried it, allowing it to join your growing pile of resentments.

This time the resentment has been manifesting itself in bitter exclamations such as:

"Why does *every* program have to have so damn much drinking?"

"Every one of my magazines is getting crammed with liquor ads! I feel like canceling my subscriptions!"

That's your anger at society, at the world at large, for allowing so much attention to alcohol, as if the removal of such attention would make your alcoholic forget his or her passion for drink! Again, because you have not known an appropriate way to express this anger, you have allowed others to feel the weight of your outbursts, of your hate and despair.

Anger at Others

What did you expect? Other people have not taken any more risks than you have been willing to take, so you have felt some righteous indignation that they haven't done anything!

What your past anger has been telling you is that, if the alcoholic's parents, ex-mates, siblings, bosses, close friends, or others had taken some sort of action, then you wouldn't have been stuck with this problem. Come now! Isn't that being a little unrealistic?

Whatever would make you think that others would have done what *you* have not been willing to do? But being human beings, the tendency to shift the blame up or down the line has continued to invade your thinking. Many times, it has taken the form of turning anger into such deep resentment that genuine hatred for your alcoholic's parents or siblings has emerged. This is a hatred that you've wondered at, a hatred that wasn't there when the relationship was still young; when the alcoholism had not yet sunk into your consciousness as the reality that it is.

You have found yourself very angry indeed that an ex-mate didn't get help in the form of treatment or, worse, that an ex-mate may have even *joined* the alcoholic in the drinking that was progressively getting out of control. Your alcoholic's parents "should have known," you tell yourself, and therefore taken some action (as yet undefined by you) to prevent the drinking from getting out of hand.

Your anger may be directed at an older brother or sister who "just let" the drinking of your loved one continue or, worse, even contributed to the problem by joining in the drinking.

Your anger has made you say in the deep, dark, ugly parts of your mind, "Why couldn't it have been *him?*" in reference to a brother of your alcoholic. The worst of it is, it might very well *also* be him, since alcoholism is a family disease. But for now, your anger is directed at the fact that others might have been able to do something and didn't.

In other words, *they*—whoever they might be—have just sat around and waited for *you* to take on the problem! They have dumped in your lap the responsibility to do something, *anything*, to make the problem go away!

Your anger at these people is even subtler. You have found yourself snapping at a mother-in-law that you have always been very fond of, a sister-in-law that has been a best buddy to you, or the kindly family doctor that always has shown such care and concern for your alcoholic. They have all suddenly become the victims of your seemingly irrational, waspish attitude.

If you are a male and are dealing with this kind of anger, you have probably found yourself comparing your "weak" partner with her "weak" mother or father and have found yourself making very unkind remarks, directly or implied, about this character defect.

The anger that you have expressed toward the other people in your alcoholic's life has been simmering for a long time. The frustrations that you have begun to feel are allowing this anger to start coming to the surface, and you have been finding yourself biting your tongue more often lately when you realized that you have been taking some cheap shots at these people because they had earlier opportunities to deal with your alcoholic's problem and didn't. It's a tough kind of anger, but you have it, and you can look back over your behavior during the past few weeks or months and see where you have created new victims of your hidden anger.

Anger at Your God

This is a deep, deep anger that isn't mentioned often enough, in my opinion. Why? Because who are we to be angry with the God of our understanding? Good question! You have probably thought that you had no right to question an unseen power in your life.

But if you are ever going to get started on the road to wellness, you will have to accept the fact that it's OK to express your anger at your God. Notice that I say, "*your* God"—not mine, or your parents', or brother's, or boss's, but *yours;* I am talking about the select God of your understanding, in whatever capacity that Infinite Being has helped you shape your life and the way you are living it.

This anger is so special that people are afraid even to talk about it; they *wail* instead! People are constantly asking me, "Why has this happened to me?" Well, if you were one of my patients, I would tell you that that word *why* is not allowed between us anymore! Instead, I would ask you to seek the how, when, where, and what of your life regarding your alcoholic. "Why," I will tell you, "belongs to an Infinite Being. What I am interested in having you ask is '*How* can I get help? *Where* can I get help? *When* can we get started? *What* are the options that are open to me?' "

Your unspoken anger at your God has arisen because you have been dwelling on the question "Why?"

"Why me?"

"Why did you (your God) let this happen to me?"

"Why did you (God) wait until I was just finding someone special to do this?"

"Why do I deserve this?"

Well, you've gotten the idea. And there simply is no use in being obsessed with the question "Why?" You have been using this anger at your God to help you continue to remain in a state of inaction. In other words, it has been pretty safe for you to drop the whole problem on God's doorstep, saying, "Why don't *you* do something about it?"

That's been a good cop-out, and you have been using it as a way to continue to feed your anger, to foster the continuation of the seven deadly sins of your past. I am very aware of how much alcoholics have made their personal God the heavy in their own dramas.

You have been walking away from your God, too! Your problem is that you have been walking away in anger, anger that has been buried just like the other four we have talked about in this chapter. Be honest! Has it *ever* crossed your mind to say, "I'm mad at *God* for this mess"? Later on this book is going to show you positive ways to handle your angers and other deadly sins. For now, we are just dealing with pointing out what you have been doing.

When your anger at your God has gotten to a boiling point, you can count on the fact that you have tried to do a little punishing of your own! How? When's the last time you were in the church or temple of your choice? When was the last time you sought some counsel from your spiritual advisor? When was the last time you passed up an opportunity to work on a particular religious project? In other words, you've done your best to *distance* yourself from the God of your understanding. That will pay back the anger you feel, won't it?

Think about the five categories of anger that have been corroding your life. With some allowances for the fact that you are a unique individual, and that it is probably impossible for us to know each other on a one-to-one basis, these five angers that I have outlined fit you! You can take a pad and pen and probably add some specialized angers of your own, and I suggest that you do that; it's healthy! What *isn't* healthy with *any* of these deadly sins of your past is to continue to bury them; to push them deeper into the recesses of your mind, turning them into cancerous resentments that are very hard to get at and to treat!

3

Your Guilt

Now that we have exposed your shame and your anger, an overpowering sense of guilt has pervaded your life. You have been letting everyone down, and mostly yourself! The dreams and ambitions that you have had for this relationship have been getting cloudier as night after night of alcoholic behaviors have been your routine.

You have been trapped by the chains of your own guilt, a guilt that flashes across the horizon of your life like a giant neon sign reading, "I have probably caused the whole thing!"

Well, it's time we looked at all that guilt, where it came from, and what has kept it around, making it easier and easier to put into action to disrupt your life. First of all, I believe that most of your guilt has been the product of what you have been subjected to and that, like most of these seven deadly sins from your past, it continues to work on you because it has become a comfortable mode in which you can operate. You have, in effect, gotten used to feeling guilty and believe that it is just going to be a regular part of your life.

In order to break the guilt down into some workable areas, let's look at three ways in which you have allowed guilt to operate so effectively in your life, in which you have convinced yourself that there never will be enough atoning for this one deadly sin.

Old Tapes from Childhood

How often can you recall the times when you took the blame for something that you really hadn't done? It seemed easier to accept the unfair punishment and have it over with than to protest your innocence and then have a long and drawn out hassle with parents, other brothers and sisters, perhaps a teacher.

These patterns of behavior are a part of your life from the time you were four or five years old and were starting to write your life script. This script is simply a way to identify the manner in which we will respond to the many problems, both physical and psychological, that will confront us in life.

Part of your own life script was to learn that guilt could make you feel absolutely terrible. Sin, bad behavior, and childhood crimes of many sorts were some of the controls that were instilled in you. If you did "something bad," it was the guilt that made you feel so terrible—more so, perhaps, than the punishment.

Old tapes from your childhood have stayed with you. If you were the caring sort of person and fit into the pattern of your family that made you the family's caretaker, then often you would step in and take the rap for a broken window or dented fender that was the work of a brother or sister. Your guilt said to you, "If I had been watching him more closely, this wouldn't have happened!"

You began to play the old guilt tape a lot. Something was telling you that it was a flaw in *your* character that caused all these so-called "bad behaviors." Therefore, you began a lifelong process of trying to become perfect, so that whatever was going wrong in your household might magically disappear.

If you had an alcoholic parent, you grew up to become an adult *child* of an alcoholic, and you are a particularly good candidate for this guilt trip! The highly respected Dr. Claudia Black, a fine lady whom I am privileged to know and call a friend, is one of this country's most knowledgeable people on the world of adult children of alcoholics. Dr. Black was elected chairperson of the National Association for Children of Alcoholics in 1984 and is herself an adult child of an alcoholic father, who died of the disease only a few years ago.

Claudia's work over the years has been published widely, and I strongly suggest you pick up a copy of her fine book, *It Will Never Happen to Me*, for more information about the guilt that has found a home with you if you are an adult child of an alcoholic.

For whatever reason, your life script has led you right up to where you are now: taking the blame for everything that has gone wrong and taking the *guilt* that accompanies such blame taking. There is something of the caretaker about you; we already know that or you would not be reading this book, would not be involved with an alcoholic, and would probably not be looking for some way to change *yourself* so that the alcoholic can get well.

You see that this old tape of yours has pretty well convinced you that, if you were just a "little better at this or that," your alcoholic would stop drinking! That's utter nonsense since alcoholism is a disease, and little or nothing that *you* do advances or retards that disease.

But you have been listening to those old guilt tapes just the same as when you have come across favorite old records from bygone eras. Have you ever done this? You are cleaning out the basement or the attic, and there, nestled among some old photo albums or other mementos, you find an old recording, perhaps of Tommy Dorsey, Frank Sinatra, or the Supremes.

Now get this. You dust off the old thing, put it on your ultramodern stereo, and play this old record. If no one is watching, you may begin to dance to the music in the same manner in which you danced way back then, with the same dance steps that you could have sworn you had long forgotten!

Slip into a classic Beatles tune, and you will find yourself rocking, just as you did back then. Your old tapes of behavior are telling you how to move your feet, even though you haven't danced that way in years! I have talked with alcoholic patients who swear they will never dance at all again because they will be all left feet without the booze to "make me limber." With a little coaxing they discover that their old tapes are still there and, once inserted into their brains again, allow the dance steps to come back even *without* the alcohol.

So the old tapes of your past behavior are still there, and you have been allowing them to play instead of replacing them with the new tapes that we will learn about together as this book progresses.

It is enough for now to believe that a lot of your guilt has come from those old childhood tapes that have kept playing. Those tapes keep saying:

"I am guilty because I failed to *do* enough!"

"I am feeling guilty because I *could have* done more!"

"I am feeling guilty because I should be a *better person!*"

As long as these tapes have continued to play, you have come to believe that your guilt was your deserved punishment.

Your Guilt as Punishment

Because you have failed in your try for perfection, it only stands to reason that you are carrying this massive burden of guilt on your shoulders as your punishment. In the past, you have been given some kind of "penance" to perform for the many "sins" you have committed.

If, as mentioned earlier, you took the blame for something you really hadn't done, then you could help smooth your guilt by getting something into the plus column, something that would make up for the things you really *had* done and weren't caught doing.

You have been accepting your guilt as the righteous punishment for the fact that you are not perfect! Now isn't that ridiculous? But sure enough, you have felt that your guilt is totally justified; that, as I told you earlier, you really had the power over the life of your alcoholic and therefore *should* feel guilty if he or she were not recovering.

Let's return to the adult child of an alcoholic for just a moment. If you are such a person, can you remember thinking that, if you got better grades or kept your room immaculate, your alcoholic parent would stop drinking?

How many times did you honestly believe that, if you could just do a little more, if you could better yourself, your alcoholic father or mother would quit the awful drinking that was so much a part of your life?

But here you are now; you *haven't* done enough, and your old tapes tell you that the guilt you are feeling is your punishment for this lack of perfection. The worst of all of this is that you believe it! It's really what you think you deserve!

So, you have accepted your guilt of the past as a just punishment for your inability to exercise all this power you thought you had to get things under control with your alcoholic. The old tapes play over and over just like those old records; the tempos and the rhythms haven't changed, and you fall right back into the same patterns of dancing to their beat, as if you were right back there in front of the bandstands of your past.

Every time an old guilt tape has played, you have responded in exactly the same way, allowing the guilt to set in more firmly than ever, because that guilt has been your punishment. Accepting *more* guilt as a natural part of your punishment for being a "failure" is the *least* you can do, isn't it?

Accepting guilt as your punishment is just like the old saying, "Do the crime; do the time!" For you, "doing the time" is only what you have come to expect and accept as your just reward for doing the crime of not being perfect.

Old Tapes from the Present

Finally, we come to the old tapes of the present that you have been using in your guilt trip. Simply stated, these old tapes have been saying, "It's all your fault!" Now that's not a news bulletin for you, since we have already brought that to your attention. But what might be new for you is to become painfully aware that you have allowed these tapes to be started in you by your alcoholic.

What's that? Do you mean that you have forgotten all

those times that you have been told that your alcoholic drinks or got drunk because of you?

Think about it! Seeking some reasons for this "fact"just might have been the reason you started the search of local bookstores. You have been told, over and over again, that it is something you are doing, or something you have failed to do, that is causing all this drinking. And the guilt that settles around those kinds of statements is absolutely crushing! It is a guilt that is augmented by those tapes of your past that we talked about in the beginning of this chapter. "It *is* something that I'm doing!" you think. It all becomes crystal clear. You have been told:

"I wouldn't drink if you were a good housekeeper!"

"If you were better in bed, I wouldn't drink so much!"

"If you *ever* cooked a decent meal, I wouldn't drink!"

"You kids are the ones that make me drink!"

"Why can't you make a decent living? No wonder I drink!"

"If you got a job, I wouldn't be so worried and drink so much!"

If I just leave the rest of these pages blank, do you think you could fill them with what you have been told are the causes of your alcoholic's drinking? I think you could. And the message here is that you have *bought* this guilt trip—hook, line, and sinker!

This is the guilt of the present, the old tapes that are playing in you right this very minute as you read this book! I know enough about your guilt as a significant other that I can picture you saying, "I shouldn't be taking the time to read! If dinner isn't ready, he'll get drunk!" or "If I had spent the money on flowers for her instead of this book, she probably wouldn't want to get drunk tonight!"

So, the old tapes from the present, combined with the old tapes of the past, just keep piling up and aligning themselves in the tape decks of your mind. A simple push of your guilt button, and they start to play; you respond to them, and you begin to dance to the tunes that they are playing and have played for years and years.

These old tapes of the present are easy to listen to, and they have become so familiar to you that it has never

occurred to you to try to replace them with new tapes—
with wellness messages, if you will.

You have allowed guilt to become a controlling factor
in your life. You have almost felt uncomfortable when you
have found yourself without guilt! It's as if an important
part of your clothing has been forgotten, as if you failed to
turn off the range before you left the house.

You have become so comfortable with your guilt that,
when it is absent for a brief period of time, you believe
part of you is missing! And guilt *has* left you for short
bursts here and there, generally when it is so patently
obvious that you were not connected with whatever happened that even *you* cannot take the blame.

Even this is not foolproof, however. I have worked
with patients who have managed to reach out and grab
guilt for events that happened hundreds of miles away! A
case in point is the woman whose husband was issued a
drunken-driving citation in his rental car in another city,
on a business trip. Her guilt button got pushed when he
said to her, "Why in the hell didn't you call me last night
at the time you said you would? I probably wouldn't have
gone down to the bar if you'd done what you said you
would!"

And she believed that.

So your guilt has wrapped around you like the burial
shroud of your emotions that it has become; you are so
used to accepting the guilt and the blame that goes with it
that it seems perfectly natural to take on more.

When the old tapes of the present are set in motion,
you resisted change of any kind. What is the reason for
this? It is because you are reconciled to coping with the
fact that it must be your fault, that your guilt is absolutely
justified.

After all, wasn't your alcoholic under control until you
came along? If he or she *did* have a problem, your tapes
say, wouldn't the abuser have done something about it?
You see, then, it has to be something that *you* either are
doing now or have done in the past to exacerbate this
awful condition!

It's so sad to realize how far you have handed out the

buttons of your emotions for other people to push. You are simply not comfortable with being free of this old-tape guilt. If someone were to take away your heavy, lead-lined boots and replace them with feather-light shoes, and then ask you to walk, you'd probably shout, "No! Give me back my heavy lead boots! I *know* how to walk in them!"

And the alcoholic in your life is ever so happy to accommodate you! Remember that the more times he can keep the focus *on you* and off his alcoholic behavior, the less threatened the alcoholic feels. When the alcoholic sees the big guilt button you are wearing, readily accessible for pushing, then push it is!

And it will work every time. You have become used to jumping into action when a word, a phrase, a glance says to you, "You're to blame!" I have seen patients who will go to almost any length to accept the blame, to feel the guilt to its most delicious fulfillment!

"I think I'm being a little irrational this time!", a significant other might say. "He wasn't *nearly* as drunk as last weekend, and I think if *I* had been in a little better mood, he might have even stayed sober."

You can see the old tape slip neatly into place in the tape deck of that woman's mind. "I'm to blame," she is saying, "and I'll watch myself next time." The tape goes on playing: "God! Why couldn't I just learn to keep my mouth shut!"

The longer the tape plays, the harder the guilt cement sets in the woman's mind. What you have been doing is just the same; you've been allowing the old tapes of the past and present to repeat over and over, fed by the guilt that you have become cozy and comfortable with in the recesses of your mind.

If you think it is difficult for the alcoholic to give up the drink, know that it is equally difficult for you to learn to give up your guilt. This is understandable because your guilt has become so logical in your thinking. It accounted for most of the feelings you carried with you through childhood and into your adult life.

Like some friendly companion, guilt has prevented you from ever passing the blame along to others for the way *they* have acted. You have selfishly accepted all the blame yourself; it has given you a feeling of power, even though that was a false feeling. What has been one of the most severe of your past seven deadly sins, guilt, will be one of the hardest to change.

But change is a must! As we proceed through this book together, perhaps you will see how you have literally allowed your guilt to prevent another person from getting well, from dealing with and putting the alcoholism into treatment and hopeful remission.

Every time you recall incidents from your past and present in which you have allowed yourself to take the blame, ask yourself how long you felt guilty about the action you either took or failed to take.

For now, let's put this deadly sin of guilt aside and move on to the next one, which has been so much a part of your past.

4

Your Denial

"I'm sure this is a *temporary* thing—you know, stress."
"It seems to me that she's *really* cutting back."
"He has a *drinking* problem, that's all."

Well, well! How many statements like these have made their way out of your mouth and into the conversation of denial? Denial has taken a terrible toll on you, the same way the other deadly sins have. It's as if you have been saying, "All this is just temporary! I know that things will be better soon."

Don't you wish! But this Land of Oz that we have called your denial has continued to haunt your past. With almost all of the significant others that I have seen in therapy, I have found a universal belief that this alcoholism is something that will go away.

With treatment, lifelong support through A.A., and continual awareness of the disease, alcoholism will be put into remission, but it will never go away! Your denial of the condition in which you find yourself has fallen into at least five categories. I'm sure that you can name others, but the five we are going to explore together are those I've seen over and over at our Gateway Treatment Center.

In the order in which you're likely to bring them up, these are the five basic types of denial.

1. "He's not *really* an alcoholic."
2. "This is a *temporary* problem."
3. "It'll get better when. . . ."
4. "There's no way I've picked an alcoholic."

32

5. "When we move to (place, job) she probably won't drink as much."

You might be thinking, "Well I never thought any of those things!" And your old tapes from the past can make you believe that you never did! Oh, the exact words or phrases might have been different, but the general idea was the same.

Denial of the disease itself and its serious impact on your lives has taken such a hold on your past as to make you believe that all the other problems of your relationship will go away if you can just get a handle on this drinking thing.

One of the things we hear at Gateway Treatment Center over and over is the couple telling us, "All of our relationship difficulties are the fault of his (her) drinking! Get rid of that, and we'll be great!"

Nothing could be further from the truth, but denial has taken another captive in the person who says that. The truth is that the alcohol has been masking a whole bunch of relationship difficulties, and when the alcohol is helped out of the picture through treatment, those problems that have always been there will pop to the surface. It's funny. You have been denying the drinking as the serious disease it is, and that has lulled you into believing that it is the only thing standing in the way of your return to the fairyland of your romance.

Many people have likened this denial of alcoholism to the same kinds of denial that you may have gone through when you lost a dear one by death: "This is just a bad dream! I'll wake up any minute now and find that he (she) isn't dead at all!"

Unfortunately, you are bitter to discover that it isn't a bad dream, that you are suddenly faced with reality of the worst kind. This denial syndrome is present in a divorce, even in a separation. You may have gone through such an experience and, if so, can remember thinking, "I didn't really go through with the divorce!" or "He didn't really *mean* it when he said he was leaving!"

The hard facts finally bring you to the realization that

you can no longer deny what has happened. You then begin a part of the healing process, a part of getting well that we require for an abundant and rich life.

The denial that you have experienced in your past, then, has been a real stumbling block to your getting well and doing something about yourself and your alcoholic.

Let's examine each of these five areas in further detail as a means of understanding better how you have allowed denial to become the deadly sin that it has.

He is Not Really an Alcoholic

You have been staring at all kinds of alcoholic behavior from the person with whom you are involved, yet denial prevents you from calling it what it is. That's understandable. If you have believed that things can change for the better if *you* just perform some major and minor miracles, then this drinking that has gotten out of hand will just go away!

Your perception of an alcoholic has been distorted perhaps by stereotypes that have been handed to us through the ages; you have grown up with a picture of the drunk, the comic figure who has been portrayed over and over in the plays and films you have seen and in the books and magazines you have read.

Therefore, if your alcoholic doesn't show any of the kinds of behavior that you have learned to associate with a drunk, how could this person be an alcoholic? All you observe is that he is drinking a lot and that you don't like what the person does when drinking. But you have been immersed in so much denial that you believe your loved one is just going through a tough time right now.

If you are really honest with yourself, you may have been excusing this behavior for many months or even years, still without having the courage to call it alcoholism. You have allowed denial to tell you that, just because he doesn't sit around with a lampshade on his head or she doesn't have her lipstick smeared all over her face, somehow it's different. Denial has been playing its old tapes through your system so strongly that you have honestly convinced yourself that maybe—no, make that *probably*—she can *learn* to drink in moderation. And rather than face the real problem, you search in vain for some way to continue to excuse the behavior that is wrecking your life.

Such wishful thinking belongs right there in the Land of Oz with some of your other behaviors of the past. For the alcoholic there is no such thing as controlled drinking or having just one or two. It just plain doesn't work that way with this disease. Yet your denial has allowed you to think along those lines.

You have steadfastly refused to look at the behavior that has been presenting itself, time after time, night after night. Ask yourself if you honestly believe that *social* drinkers start their work day with a can of beer or a shot of vodka, skillfully (sometimes *not* so skillfully) masked in a glass of orange juice.

Oh, you have heard how stressful things are at the office or how the big contract is getting everyone down. You've allowed yourself to accept almost any excuse as a reason to continue to feed your denial that the drinking has been getting stronger and longer. Long after that contract has been closed, long after the office crisis has passed, your alcoholic continues to sit in your living room or at your kitchen table, night after night, getting firmly smashed!

But *you* are not involved with an alcoholic!

This is a Temporary Problem

If all the dynamics of your denial have been working to lead you to the conclusion that you couldn't possibly be involved with an alcoholic, it only stands to reason that your thinking has said, "This is a temporary problem."

It's perfectly natural for your denial to have led you to this feeling. If your loved one is *not* alcoholic, then this thing that has come between you will just go away. The track that this form of denial leads you to is the one that makes you continue to excuse all the obvious signs of alcoholism, hoping that the thing will pass and that your life will return to normal.

So what you have done is try even harder to change *your* life, the way that *you* do things, looking for the one clue that will make this "temporary" condition pass. If your alcoholic has been complaining about lousy food, then you are suddenly becoming a little Julia Child, setting one gourmet meal after another on your table, only to have those meals treated with the same disrespect as before.

If the principal complaint has been messy housekeeping, then it doesn't matter how tired *you* may be from your own hard day's work. There we find you, running the vacuum again, sometimes at really odd hours. I once treated a significant other whose seven deadly sins had been so firmly entrenched that she waited about six years into her husband's sobriety to start getting up at one in the morning to vacuum! She was making up for lost time, punishing herself for possibly having stopped or hindered his getting well because she wasn't keeping their house clean enough!

Since your denial has led you to believe that alcoholism is temporary, you will try almost anything to come up with the winning formula to end the temporary insanity that has taken hold of your loved one. Alas! Alcoholism is *never* temporary. There is *no cure;* there is only remission of the disease.

The more your denial allows you to consider this a temporary condition, the more time you waste, not taking any definitive action to get help for you and your alcoholic. This has been a denial of your past. It must not be allowed to be an active tape of your present or future!

It'll Get Better When. . . .

You can easily see how all these phases of denial tie together and how you have probably experienced all of them in one form or another. If you have believed that the conditions you have been witnessing are only temporary, then it's pretty obvious that you have played a denial tape that tells you "things will get better when. . . ." The problem is that you keep inserting new things into your life to make the "when" happen, and it never does! As we just learned, if you keep a pretty clean house, you try to keep a cleaner house; when that doesn't stop the drinking, you say, "Things'll get better *when* I can hire a housekeeper and I won't have to spend my time cleaning." As you read this, you might even be chuckling to yourself, realizing how warped that kind of thinking is but that it is exactly the kind of behavior you have been exhibiting.

Your denial can take very strange turns in your road. "Things'll get better when we get the new car and the old one isn't always breaking down." Why is this? The alcoholic has given "that damn car" as the reason for excessive drinking because it caused all the stress and anxiety of his or her day.

So you have been working extra hours, saving money more than ever or perhaps seriously talking to banks and loan companies, trying to figure out a way to get the new car that you know deep down you can't afford. But you continue to convince yourself that this (temporary) condition will get better *when* you remove the old car as a source of difficulty for your drinker.

I remember the case of the woman who had played this denial tape so strongly that she narrowed down her "things'll get better when" to her children.

"Yep!" she told me, "things'll get better for Mickey and me when Kevin and Terri are off in college."

"What makes that so?" I asked.

"Mickey can't get any studying done himself on his master's degree with them in the house. So he drinks a 'little more' than he should to quiet his nerves from all the noise."

"Well, you know what happened. Kevin and Terri *did* head off for college; Mickey continued to drink, harder than ever, and dropped his master's program. Our patient was absolutely convinced then that "things'll get better when Mickey can build a study just for himself to *really* be able to concentrate."

She borrowed money on their house, hired a contractor, and converted their large garage into a really wonderful study/den area that was contained above the cars. It was a showplace in which he could work and study and get the master's degree that was preoccupying his life.

When this patient discovered empty vodka bottles hidden all over her husband's study, she knew the painful truth. All of her denial tapes about things getting better "when" had just been smoke screens. It was this final breaking of her illusion that led the couple into treatment and eventual recovery.

I have seen that woman since, and the study is now truly utilized for all sorts of wonderful things for both her husband Mickey and her. She has entered college to work on the undergraduate degree she always wanted, and now that her husband is in recovery, they are sharing moments *together*, no longer playing her old denial tapes!

There's No Way I've Picked an Alcoholic

This denial tape is one of vanity, *your* vanity, getting in the way of getting well. You have been a wise shopper; you were the "bargain finder" of the family when you were growing up. You have demonstrated over and over that you have good common sense. Therefore, you simply could *not* have selected an alcoholic for your serious relationship! You see, this helps feed your denial that the person really *is* an alcoholic. If you couldn't be "dumb enough" (I've heard that a million times!) to pick an alcoholic, then obviously your special person *isn't* one. Makes sense to you, right?

This denial tape plays so strongly that when you are presented with hard-core evidence of alcoholism in your love you have refused to believe it. You refuse to believe because it would put a radical hole in the image you have maintained of having good sense, having great judgment, and being able to pick winners.

If winning and being "right" has always been a part of your formative years, then it stands to reason that you have convinced yourself that you have still tied up with a winner. The problem is that that winner seems to be on a losing streak with alcohol!

A lady in hospital treatment where I was doing a lecture told all of us in the room of being asked to watch that her father didn't fall asleep (from too much booze!) at the dinner table and to make sure "his head didn't drop into the mashed potatoes!"

Well, you can imagine that the whole room burst into laughter. But the lady quickly overcame the laughter by saying, "But my father was *no alcoholic!*"

"Why do you believe that, Mona?" I asked.

"Because," she replied in a suitably righteous tone, "My mother didn't *allow* any alcoholics in her house!"

Well, Mona and the rest of the assembled patients all discussed how believing that her mother would never *choose* an alcoholic had become an absolute fact, in spite of much evidence about her father's long-term alcoholism. Mona herself had fallen into the same trap as her mother. Not only was *she* alcoholic, but she had chosen an alcoholic for a mate, one who was still actively drinking.

This woman was in treatment for *her* problem, but she strongly denied that her husband was little more than a "heavy drinker," a denial tape she continued to play even after her own treatment program at the hospital was concluded.

Mona insisted she simply was *not* involved with an alcoholic for much the same reasons her mother wasn't; mother and daughter simply would never *choose* one!

This denial tape, fed by vanity, by a sense of infallibility in making life choices, can be so strong as to prevent the seeking of help for either of the people involved, for long periods of years.

You may be one of those persons, deluding yourself that you could ever have made a wrong move in tying up with an alcoholic. Your foolish pride has gotten squarely in the way of your past. It continues in your present and certainly will be a detrimental factor in your future. Bad tape! Terrible denial!

When We Move to (Place, Job) He (She) Probably Won't Drink as Much!

This denial tape is a lot like number three, but it's more geographic in nature. That's why we'll call this denial the "geographic escape" tape. Simply stated, it means that you have believed in the past that a physical relocation of you and your alcoholic will cure the problem.

A young couple sat in our offices several years ago and went through a standard first interview to assess whether alcohol had become a problem in their life. Over and over, their behavior was confronted, and it became painfully obvious to them and the therapist that alcohol was indeed a culprit in their young lives and that he was very probably an alcoholic.

The "geographic escape" tape got slipped into the "play" position by the man's wife, who seriously intoned to me, "We are planning to move to California. I think he'll be better there!"

That couple, I am proud to say, shares that story with new members of our program in treatment, when graduates from treatment are invited back to share recovery experiences as an aid to those who are just beginning.

It's one of the biggest laugh-getters for them, because regardless of how ludicrous it now seems to think that a geographic move would leave the alcohol problem where it was, they gave it deadly serious consideration at the time.

Think back to your own geographic escapes and how you have used them as a means of furthering your own denial about the real problems facing you.

Perhaps you have focused on how a move to another state, coupled with a new job, will solve the problem. Many times you have even considered leaving the relationship in a vain attempt to "save" your alcoholic—as if *your* moving to another city, or another state, or even another apartment or house would allow you magically to take the problem with you!

Yet your denial tape here has been so strong that you have convinced yourself it would be for "the good of all" if you simply packed up and left, and of course, carried the dreaded disease out the door with you.

You can remember instances of your own geographic escapes and how you plotted to bring them about, fruitlessly believing that a move of one kind or another was the answer to your alcoholic problems.

These five areas of denials undoubtedly have been a part of your past behavior. They have permeated the darkest reaches of your mind and your body, making denial one of the deadliest of the seven sins. Denial has kept you off track for long periods of time, prevented you from taking the actions that are so necessary to change the course of your life as the significant other person in the life of an alcoholic.

Denial must not be allowed in your present or in your future, but we are looking at your past. If you have seen the ways that your denial has been ever present, if you have been able to identify with some of the ways in which this deadly sin has been taking its toll on you, then you have taken an important step in your own recovery!

Remember that the denial you have been experiencing in the past has been a protective device, albeit harmful, keeping you from the final truth. That truth, of course, is the fact that alcoholism is in your life, probably has been there for some time, and probably will remain there unless and until you take measures to begin the recovery process along with your alcoholic.

In the next chapter, we will look at how these previous four deadly sins have contributed to number five—fear!

5

Your Fear

It's easy to understand how this next deadly sin has been a part of your past. You have seen how shame, anger, guilt, and denial have controlled your life and have led you quite naturally to this.

It is *fear*. You have allowed yourself to become practically immobilized by the fear that nothing you can do will help, the fear that whatever you might decide to do will fail, and, the most awesome fear of all, the fear that it might already be too late.

That's why this deadly sin falls so readily into place behind the other sins that we have been exploring together. But I think it's helpful if, as for the other behaviors you have been practicing in your past, we break down this fear into more workable categories.

If we were to look at what has made fear such a controlling force in your past, I believe we would find that you have been subject to four types of fear:

1. fear of discovery
2. fear of taking action
3. fear of reprisal
4. fear of the future

As in all of our discussions of the seven deadly sins of your past, there may be other categories of fear that you have felt. However, as a therapist, I have seen enough significant-other patients to know these four fears are common to almost all of you. It's always interesting to hear from you, the readers of my books, when you send me new, different, or absolutely unique experiences that you have encountered in dealing with alcoholism. I add them to my own experiences as helpful tools in treating the disease in other people.

So, whether your fears match my list or not isn't important; what *is* important is to recognize that you have allowed yourself to be the victim of these fears. Let's look at them in more detail.

Fear of Discovery

This old fear tape is the one that suddenly hits you right square in the eyes, at the moment that the last vestiges of your denial have withered off the vines of your false hopes. The fear of discovery tape says to you, "This is it! This is *really* an *alcoholic* that you're involved with!" And the tape carries a frightening message that says that all this time you have been kidding yourself into thinking that maybe, just maybe, it *wasn't* alcoholism.

The fear of discovery is the same kind of fear that may have struck many soldiers or other servicepeople when the doors of the landing craft slammed down on some foreign beach. It is the fear that tells you this is no dress rehearsal, this is the real thing.

The fear of discovery is like stage fright that finally strikes even the seasoned performer, usually when he is least expecting it. It is the sudden fear of realization that whatever you have been denying is really happening.

In your past dealings with the alcoholic, you have been investing a great deal of time, energy, and no doubt money into the theory that your problem was severe but *not* alcoholic. But when you finally own up to the problem, when you finally make the discovery, and the last veils have fallen from your face, the fear of discovery can be devastating!

You have allowed yourself a certain luxury of believing that this drinking situation was something that was not going to reach a serious or critical point. When it does, you essentially have not been prepared for it. What you have done to deal with this fear of discovery is, frankly, *nothing*.

You have simply crawled deeper into your bed, pulled your covers tighter around your head, and *hoped* that this discovery of yours would turn out to be wrong. You have played ostrich by burying your head in the sands of your life, and that's what has made fear one of your seven deadly sins of past behavior.

If this were any other disease, cancer for example, you would have gone through the same kinds of awful terror associated with the discovery of the disease. But then you would have started to do something about it! Unfortunately, in the case of alcoholism, your fear, although of immense proportion when the discovery is made, is quickly plunged back into the sands and covered over by new denial tapes that help the anxiety pass from your vision. You have literally reburied the fear of discovery by finding new methods of denying its existence.

Fear of Taking Action

This is, of course, a natural consequence of the fear just outlined. What is the element that has stopped you dead in your tracks, preventing you from doing something about the problem? It is, quite simply, the fear of failure. It's not even a guaranteed failure, but one that *might* happen, and that's enough to prevent you from taking action.

We could almost retitle this fear the fear of failure, but there are some important pieces of this fear tape that transcend just failure. One of those pieces is the fact that you have been positive that any action you might take will result in a loss.

Not only might you lose the relationship, but you have still been caught in the old tapes of your belief that you have a lot of power over someone else's life, and you have felt that you might honestly cause a death if you took any action that separated the alcohol-abusing person from his or her bottle! This fear, then, has prevented you from really taking action involving doctors, hospitals, treatment centers, etc., because you have bought the idea that the person you love will literally die if he or she is removed totally from alcohol.

So you allow this fear of taking action to run its merry way as a rather well-known melody on your tape machine! Another piece of the failure to take action fear tape is the one that tells you, "You don't have the right to interfere."

Boy, is that a toughie! One part of you is screaming out to take the power and do something, and the other side—unfortunately, it's the one you have been listening to—says, "For God's sake, keep your hands off!" So, you listen to the tape of your fear of taking action and do nothing. That's what has kept you in the neutral position on the gear shift of your life.

You have continued to play this fear tape, always promising yourself that you'll do something when the problem gets bad enough. But you have made damn sure that you have never recognized the problem as bad enough to force you into action. That's because *denial* has been working hand in glove with your fear.

Fear of Reprisal

This portion of your overall submission to the sin of your fear concerns itself with what you think will happen to you if you *were* to confront the problem *and* take action against it. We are, after all, creatures who want to survive. That desire for survival makes us do anything at all to protect our chances of living the way we want to live.

When this tape has been playing in you, however, it has said that other forces outside your control will take some revenge on you for what you are doing to the alcoholic. This fear of reprisal can, in turn, be divided into subcategories:

- fear of reprisal from your family
- fear of reprisal from the alcoholic's family
- fear of reprisal from friends to whom you've looked for support

Reprisal from Your Family

The first one is a strange duck indeed, but one that I've heard expressed more times than I care to count. It is the reprisal fear tape that has your family telling you that, if you do something about the alcoholic problem in your life, you will cast shame on your family!

You may have been thinking of the threat of a separation or divorce from your alcoholic as a means of impressing him or her with the seriousness of the problem and its effect on your relationship. But the family reprisal fear tape gets played quickly, loudly, and, unfortunately, effectively in too many cases.

You do nothing in response to this tape, which tells you things like "There's never been a separation or divorce in our family!" or "Think of *us*! What are *we* supposed to say when everyone finds out?"

Of course these are generally the same family members who have no trouble at all covering up when their son-in-law, daughter, or whoever is falling down drunk in front of friends and neighbors! But the thought of that person and *you* getting some kind of treatment help or being seen at Al-Anon and A.A. meetings is just too much for the family to handle! The fear of reprisal tape rolls on.

Reprisal from the Alcoholic's Family

The next subcategory is reprisal from the alcoholic's family, and this is somewhat similar, though not identical, to what you've heard in the tape played from your own family.

One principal difference is that anything that you might consider doing is fed back to you as *interference* with the family! It doesn't matter if you are the devoted wife, husband, long-time friend, or roommate. If you do something, the reprisal from the alcoholic's family says you will be cut off for interfering! This is a particularly devastating fear tape if you have no immediate family of your own. The thought of being ostracized from your family-by-marriage or your "adopted family" is too much for you to bear! So, once again, you have done nothing. You have capitulated to the deadly sin of Fear.

You may have been praised by your alcoholic's mother or father as being "more of a daughter to us than a daughter-in-law." The fear of reprisal from the family of the alcoholic is awesome in its capacity to keep you in bondage.

Reprisal from Friends

The third subcategory of the fear of reprisal is the one that comes from the friends of both you and your alcoholic, who somehow manage to indicate to you that they don't want to get involved with the problem. They have told you that "our friendship and our love for you both" would be "threatened" if they were to participate in, say, an intervention with your alcoholic.

They have given strong indications to you that, if you somehow took some definitive action to help get the alcoholic into treatment or A.A., it could "break up the old gang"; you know, "just tear us all apart!" And because we are creatures that most often run in packs throughout our lives, you have considered this fear of reprisal from friends to be a significant enough threat to allow you to do nothing once again.

This fear tape is not unlike the one played to the newly separated or divorced person who suddenly wonders why the telephone doesn't ring anymore for bridge or tennis or just a cup of coffee. Your friends, faced with the possibility that you will be threatening their right to drink, want no part of whatever it is you might be planning to do for your alcoholic.

This is, of course, not a blanket indictment of all of your friends. I use it as an example of one of the fears that very possibly has kept you locked in its grip. It becomes another nail in your coffin of fears, though, if you have been the kind of person that thought you could count on a particular friend or group of friends to help.

Alcoholism and the problems associated with it can be a very firm dividing line among friends. It is a very personal disease, a fact that often causes friends and families to look at themselves and find a parallel in their own behaviors. This causes them to reinforce that they want to be counted out in any such action you might want to take to get help for your alcoholic. It's just too close to home in many instances!

Fear of the future

Finally, we look at one of the most deeply rooted of your fears of the past. You have been afraid to face the future, to take the risks necessary to change your life and that of your alcoholic. This fear of the future also has three subcategories:

- fear of being alone
- fear of making the same mistake
- fear of being isolated from others

Fear of Being Alone

We all dislike being alone. The alcoholic has a particular penchant for not wanting to be alone. And you have not wanted a future alone, in most cases, and the thought that you might end up as a solo act has prevented you from taking action to make any changes in the way you are living and tolerating alcoholism.

You have listened to this tape and its siren song that tells you it's better to put up with this than to be alone. What a shame! Yet thousands upon thousands of significant-other people play this fear tape every day of their miserable lives. The real tragedy is that they soon fall victim to this siren song, and before long they aren't miserable anymore.

This is where you may have also landed in your fear plunge, and it has taken hold of you. What misery you may have endured seems better than the misery of being alone.

The fear of being alone is different from actually being alone. All of us cherish some time when we can be by ourselves, and we often get very protective of such moments in our lives. This is not, however, the type of thing that causes the fear you have allowed to rule your life. You have been afraid to spend your life alone. The problem has been that you have failed to recognize that life with an active alcoholic is pretty much like spending life alone!

Think about it! How many times have you been nothing more than just a baby-sitter to your passed-out loved one? How many times have you ended up the evening just like you started it—alone by the TV? How often have you found yourself attending a particular function alone because your alcoholic was unable to pull herself together in time?

Yet you have been afraid to be alone, so you have once again taken no action to get well.

Fear of Making the Same Mistake

The second fear of the future that you have endured— rather, *nurtured*—in your past has been the fear that you will make the same mistake; that is, that you will end up with another alcoholic. Considering the statistic I shared with you earlier in this book, that two out of three females who lose an alcoholic to death or by divorce will end up with another alcoholic, gives credence to your fears!

Without treatment, you will very possibly become one of those statistics. Men often repeat their mistakes as well, but not in as great numbers as females. Females are more security oriented, and therefore seem willing to "try another" drinker, if only to provide themselves and possibly their children, with a place to call "home." Even more depressing for you is to understand that this fear of the future seems to lock you even more firmly into an alcoholic relationship if you are female. Nine out of ten women will stay with an alcoholic male, while only one of ten men will stay with an alcoholic female. You have only to look at your friends who, like you, may be locking themselves more and more tightly into an alcoholic relationship, to see that this fear of the future tape that says, "I might just get rid of this alcoholic and end up with another!" plays louder and louder as the days, weeks, and months go by.

Rather than go through the agony of making the same mistake, you have chosen to deal with the mistake that you already have in your possession! This fear has placed a warrant on your life, one that daily claims payments for its existence.

"At least I know what to expect!" you find yourself saying, and the tragedy goes on.

Fear of Being Isolated from Others

The last of the fears of the future that have been a part of your past is the one that makes you afraid that you will be isolated from those you love if somehow you choose to take some get-well action. This has a strong tie-in to the fear of reprisal from family and friends, but it rates some separate consideration because of a unique quality. It may just end up being *you* who chooses the isolation!

Your fear has been so deeply rooted that you will go back and allow the other deadly sins, particularly shame and guilt, drive you into isolating yourself so you don't have to deal with explanations or endless excuses for what has happened or what has *not* happened.

You have chosen this hermitlike existence as a means of escaping, yet it is a trap of fear in itself. If you have always been an outgoing person—cheerful, witty perhaps— you are afraid to let others see that this alcoholism has taken a terrible toll on you, so you know you will have to become withdrawn.

Rather than do that, rather than have to undergo such a change in your personality, you have allowed the fear of such isolation to be dominant. You have decided you can't take the chance. Treatment, Al-Anon, A.A., all go by the wayside because this fear of the future tape plays so strongly; it has become your master and you its slave!

So this deadly sin of Fear, falling as it does after the others we have discussed, takes a very firm root in your past. It has continued to be nurtured through all of your days, weeks, months, or years of living with an alcoholic.

You have tolerated all the torment and agony of life with an alcoholic who is actively drinking because of having been afraid to make changes in your life. You have chosen never to open the doors in your life because you may encounter all sorts of wild animals behind those doors. For shame!

6

Your Failure to Take
Risks

It has always been easy for you to follow what others have already accomplished. You have not been the trail-blazer that is required in this business of getting well, and this has made you the victim of your sixth of the seven deadly sins.

You have simply not been willing to take the risks necessary to start you and your alcoholic on the long road to recovery. Over and over, you have poised yourself on the brink of risk taking, only to pull back from the edge and climb back down from the high diving boards of your life. What makes this happen, anyhow?

You have allowed yourself to remain in the state of unwellness you have been in because you have been afraid of facing change in your life. Over and over, I tell patients in therapy with us that they must "always go for the brass rings" of life. My four kids have heard their dad exhort them to go for it for as long as we could communicate, particularly after my own sobriety became the reachable goal for us all.

But you! Not only have you failed in the past to go for the brass ring; you have not even wanted to get on the carousels of your life! If you think I am being unduly harsh, it's because I have seen so many significant others fall into the deadly sin trap and stay there, like some struggling fly, watching helplessly while the spider of alcoholism inches toward them, devouring all in its way.

You have failed to look around you and imagine a better world for yourself. You have stopped short of the risk taking that involves changes in your life because you have become strangely comfortable with your life, as horrendous as it may have become.

It's only natural that this is so. To take a risk might be, after all, to succeed, and you have been as afraid to succeed as you have been to continue to fail! So you've been living on a teeter-totter, balancing in the middle, not giving the extra push necessary to rise farther but afraid you will come plummeting down to hard ground below!

At our treatment center a sheet of paper is thumbtacked to the bulletin board in the coffee room. This page is entitled "Risks," and it has no known author. It is such a favorite that hardly a week passes without a request for a copy of it.

Here it is, just for *you* to ponder.

RISKS

To laugh is to risk appearing the fool.
To weep is to risk appearing sentimental.
To reach out for another is to risk involvement.
To expose feelings is to risk exposing your true self.
*To place your ideas, your dreams, before a crowd is
    to risk their loss.*
To love is to risk not being loved in return.
To live is to risk dying.
To hope is to risk despair.
To try is to risk failure.

*But risks must be taken, because the greatest hazard
    in life is to risk nothing.*
*The person who risks nothing does nothing, has
    nothing, and is nothing.*
*They may avoid suffering and sorrow, but they
    cannot learn, feel, change, grow, love, live.*
*Chained by their attitudes, they are a slave, they
    have forfeited their freedom.*
Only a person who risks is free.

I hope that you will make a copy of this and keep it somewhere to remind you on a daily basis what effect risk taking—and, particularly, the *lack* of risk taking—has had on your life. If you have been a reader of mine before, you will know that *my* favorite place to put up "stuff to live by" is the refrigerator door. I don't have little kids around anymore, bringing their school papers home to adorn the fridge door, but old habits die hard! That's where I kept things I cared about for years, and that's where I keep things like this now.

The old tapes of your life have led you in such a circle that every time it appeared possible for you to take a risk in your life you found a way to back off. A friend and colleague of mine, Dr. William Simon, along with his psychologist wife, Marilyn, addressed a conference I attended a couple of years ago.

Bill and Marilyn organized everyone in the room into long rows facing each other, one on one. As each of us stood opposite a stranger, the Simons began some intense risk-taking communications that we were to engage in with the partner opposite. The questions and responses were intimate and sexual in nature since this was a workshop for therapists dealing with sexuality.

Bill told us, "Every time you are afraid to take a risk in your life, ask yourself, 'How long will I be dead?'"

That's an eye-opening question. You have failed to take risks, but what is the thing that has stopped you? The worst thing I can imagine is to wonder what *might* have been in your life. You have failed to take risks in your life, thus wasting a large part of it. This doesn't mean that you should carry on in reckless abandon, not caring what or who gets hurt in the process of your risk taking. It does mean, however, that your fear has kept you from making the necessary moves to *confront* the problem, *act* on the problem, and *change* the way you continue to *live* with the problem!

If you won't throw bait in the water, you can't expect to catch a fish! This old tape of yours has simply caused you to continue to live in misery, even when faced with the results of living with all the other deadly sins we have been discussing.

Look to your childhood. Were you the one who never

answered the "I dare yous" of growing up? Maybe. Probably. Since your life script has been in place since you were four or five years old, the chances are pretty good that you didn't do a whole bunch of risk taking during your formative childhood years.

A recent film, *A Christmas Story*, was a wonderful example of daring and risk taking. The young boy whose story was told in it recalls the extent to which he and his playmates were challenged. I don't remember it exactly, but he detailed all the growing elements of the dares of his childhood. A simple "I dare you" wasn't so bad, but when it got to a "triple-dog-dare you," that was *serious* stuff! Anyone who didn't answer a "triple dog dare" threat couldn't expect to save face ever again!

You have been trying to save face, but you haven't been taking any risks. Over and over, you have considered confronting, acting, or changing the way you have been living your life. Just as quickly, however, you have rejected taking any of those steps because you have been afraid of the risks that were involved.

After all, confronting the problem of alcoholism is to risk admitting its existence, breaking through the great stone wall of denial. Acting on the problem means you might have to risk a series of encounters with treatment professionals, A.A., Al-Anon and face your friends and family as well as yourself.

Changing your life means you might take the risk of getting well, and, whether you believe it or not, you have grown very comfortable with being sick. You may be very unhappy with my suggestion that you are sick, but it's the truth! You continue to live with a sick problem, in a sick environment, and, as a result, you yourself have become just as sick as the person that is the identified patient for treatment.

You have, in short, failed to get on the carousel of your life because it will show you the brass ring of wellness, ready to be grabbed. You have been afraid of not reaching that ring, of *failing* in its quest, and therefore have chosen never to put yourself in a position of having to reach. No one can ever "triple dog dare" you if you never engage in the games of life in which those challenges might be offered. Rather than face the risk, you have declined to play the game at all.

All of your past deadly sins are so interwoven that it is impossible to deal with one and not the others. This sin of non-risk taking is no exception. It has been ever present when you were playing the old tapes of your shame. You continued to hide your involvement with an alcoholic, something that was probably patently obvious to everyone else, because the risk might be the loss of friends, family members, or the alcoholic.

The risk factor has been so great for you in playing through the old tape of your anger that you have spent years perhaps in burying that anger in the vast garbage bag of your body. It has just been sitting there, fermenting, making you miserable. But rather than take the risk of allowing your anger to come forth, be answered, and be treated, you have continued to live, burying more and more within you, bloating your emotional life until you believe you will literally explode.

The sin of your guilt has kept you from risk taking on an even more substantial basis. In this case, any risk you might take simply reinforces the idea that you have been guilty. It's admitting to something, and that prevents you from coming forth, from 'fessing up to the problem and getting rid of the old guilt tapes that have been playing for so long.

We have already discussed how your denial has prevented risk taking. You have continued to foster this great denial, and it has worked! It has allowed you to avoid doing much, if any, risk taking. After all, you have reasoned, "if there really isn't any problem, why should I take any risks?"

Makes sense to me! Worse than that, it has *really* made sense to you. So on you go, day after day, week after week, month after month, steeped in denial and avoiding making decisions that have built-in risk factors. You have allowed this routine of listening to your old tapes march you right past the playground, past the carousel, and past the brass ring! Worse than that, you have begun to believe that this is how *everyone* lives their lives, content without risks.

One of the most satisfying events—perhaps the greatest—that my partner Paul and I have at our Gateway Treatment Center is graduation night. All of the families who have completed their six months of intensive outpatient care gather in front of the people currently in treatment. We turn the night over to them, encouraging them to tell the new people about their feelings—how it was when they first entered treatment, how working with the staff felt, what it has been like getting well together.

Paul and I stand in the back of the room or just outside the door with the rest of our wonderful staff and listen to the significant others talk about "how scared I was to take the risk of getting well for myself!" It's wonderful! The shy, almost cowering young mother; the older man who thought he was being "a wonderful guy" to put up with his alcoholic wife; the teenager afraid to admit he had an alcoholic mother—all standing there and sharing their risks and the rewards that have come to them in six months worth of risk taking.

Almost all of these people will tell their audience that denial was a big factor in preventing them from getting well. Male and female significant others alike will speak of "how often I skirted the issue, thinking it wasn't a big damn deal!"

For you, that old bugaboo of your denial has "jes kept rollin' along!" to parody "Old Man River." You can easily see how one old tape of your past has linked itself to another old tape, forging an endless chain that, instead of rescuing you, only binds you tighter and tighter, preventing you from taking the necessary risks in your life.

The past sin of your fear contributes likewise to the failure to take risks. We know that several kinds of fear have been at work on your emotions, as we discovered in Chapter 5. Looking more closely at the tapes of your fear, is it any wonder that you have failed to take risks in your life? If the present and existing conditions in your past life have been keeping you trudging through your life in fear, then what, you ask yourself, would ever possess you to risk making changes?

You may have considered just chucking the whole thing and making the scariest and most radical change of all: filing for separation or divorce. And yet your old tape of fear has persisted and you have bypassed the risk taking in favor of the known fear that you have learned to live with.

One of my favorite quotes for people who are afraid to take risks in their lives comes from *The Confucian Analects*. The ancient philosopher once said, "The way out is via the door. How is it that nobody recognizes this method?"

The way out of so many of your past sins is through the door of risk taking! It can, as for Dorothy of Oz fame, suddenly open from a drab black-and-white setting to one of color, magic, excitement, and beauty!

Am I advocating, then, that all of you run right out and file for separation or divorce? Of course not! But I *am* suggesting that you may have automatically shunned even *thinking* about such actions as a means of emphasizing the seriousness of the alcoholic problem for both of you.

Failure to take the risk of even *considering* such a drastic measure may have painted you into a corner of your life where no one can reach you. A few months ago I was a guest on a radio talk show that had listeners call in with questions about alcoholism. One woman, calling from a distant city, literally rejected every possibility that I was able to suggest as a means of taking action to get help for herself and her alcoholic husband. Separation and divorce were "strictly" against her religion. She "couldn't get anything out of Al-Anon"; she didn't think they could afford treatment, even though I was prepared to give her the names of several public or pay-as-you-can programs. She had an excuse for everything! This poor creature had allowed fear to make *any* kind of risk taking for herself and her husband an impossibility.

Even more tragic was a recent case I had become involved in, without even any hands-on experience with the case. It was a weekend in which I was the therapist on call for our Gateway Treatment Center.

A friend and I had gone to a movie that we had both been waiting to see. About 20 minutes before the end of the picture, my pager alerted me that a crisis call was holding. I left my seat and made the call. Our answering service had kept the distraught female on the line, and I was patched directly through to her.

Her husband was drunk and had beaten her and the children, and there was a loaded gun in the house. I asked her where her husband was, and she said he had passed out on the couch. She was in obvious fear, not only for herself, but for her children.

"You must take your children and leave the house immediately," I said. "Can you go to a relative's house or to a friend's place?" She said she couldn't leave; she couldn't drive the family truck.

I asked her for her address, and she immediately became as hysterical as she could without taking the chance of awakening her drunken husband.

"No! No!" she cried to me. "You'll call the police! If you send the police, he will beat me and the children more!"

Try as I might, I could not get her address, and calling the police was exactly what I intended to do, believing that there was a clear and present danger to all concerned in that household. The lady told me she had called the police once before, and her husband had *really* beaten her and the children after the police had left. Oh, he had waited for a few days, but he *had* done it!

While I was talking to the distraught woman, our phone operators were having the call traced for me, as is the custom in an emergency situation. The woman became more fearful, begging me to do something but tying my hands at every step of the way.

The last words I heard from her were "He's awake! He may have the gun!" And she hung up. We had by then gotten the telephone number and the address from which the call was being made. The police were dispatched, and the situation was in their hands. Since the woman never contacted us again, nor did I read of any shooting in the next day's paper, I could only conclude the incident was handled as another "domestic quarrel." The husband is, very likely, still out there getting drunk on a regular basis, and the woman is still doing nothing to allow her to be helped.

I use this anecdote to illustrate that past tapes of fear, justified in this case, *still* can prevent a significant other from doing the risk taking that can be so essential to the safety of people like this woman and her children.

What did she have to lose by taking the risk of letting me help her? Certainly less than what she had experienced at the hands of her drunken husband in the past. But, you see, she had *survived* that incident. She knew how to *cope* with that particular hurt. It was the fear of what she *didn't* know that made the risk impossible. My guess is that she will continue to tolerate this beastly behavior; it's something she has become used to; change was something foreign to her. Her failure to take risks was chaining her to God-knows-what. She might have been referred to a mental health agency and to a shelter for battered women, but whether she would pursue either avenue was doubtful.

Over and over, you can examine the past tapes of your life and see where you have let many opportunities to take risks pass you by. Even the simplest of actions has many times gone unfulfilled because you would not even consider taking the risk necessary to make those actions come into play in your life.

You may have considered that the risk you took to begin the relationship you are now in was enough; that, by God, you will sink or swim with the cards fortune has dealt you. The thing you have consistently failed to realize in dealing with alcoholism is that risk taking becomes a valuable tool in the potential for treatment, for help, for recovery!

If you have considered that you have reached the end of your rope, then what prevents you from trying another rope? If you believe that you have exhausted your patience "with this woman" or "given this guy all the chances in the world," then what in heaven's name has been stopping you from considering courses of action that might involve high risk?

It has been your incredible tie-in with all the past deadly sins that seems to outweigh any possibility to consider risk taking in any form. You have played those old tapes for such a long time that they don't even *seem* like the wrong courses of action anymore! You have actually allowed yourself to believe that some miracle is going to occur that will take all the decisions out of your hands and leave you free from having to take any risks at all.

Risk taking is an option that has been available to you all along, but your insecurity about a life that might hold new problems, challenges, and opportunities for wellness simply has been stronger than the desire to make any change that risk taking might suggest.

Aren't you tired of knowing that you have been getting mired more deeply into this quagmire of despair? When is the last time you took yourself to the playgrounds and watched children sliding down the slides, riding the swings higher and higher, challenging the jungle gyms, or simply running, laughing, and playing, taking risk after risk with seemingly carefree abandon?

Haven't you wanted to join them? Haven't you wanted to climb on the carousel and ride that big horse, the one over there next to the edge where it's easier to reach out and grab the brass rings?

What's stopping you? Go for it! Your failure to take risks has kept you chained long enough!

7

Your "Enabling" Behavior

My guess is that most of you have found it easier to continue doing nothing about your past six sins than to take any action at all. Some of you may have read this far and decided to make some changes in your life, to take some risks. But assuming that you remain with the majority, you have found it more to your liking to continue the practice of "enabling."

What is "enabling," anyhow? In alcoholism—in fact, in most areas of human behavior—enabling is the process through which you have failed to take some action or series of actions that could help the alcoholic person realize the consequences of alcoholic behavior.

Let's bring this practice down to a simple example, that of child rearing. If you have a small child who is, say, reaching up and pulling things off the coffee table onto the floor, that is probably unacceptable behavior.

But suppose that every time he does that stunt, you simply pick up the objects and place them back in their proper place. You neither scold nor reprimand the child in any forceful way.

What, pray tell, is ever going to show that child that pulling things off the table is unacceptable? He will continue this kind of behavior, and you will have continued to *enable* him to do so without his realizing any consequences.

It is the same with your alcoholic. You have continued, in your past at least, to enable your alcoholic to continue exactly what she has been doing: drinking without feeling any consequences. In my book, *Sitting in the*

Bay Window (Contemporary Books, Inc., 1984), I discuss how parents are the classic enablers when dealing with their young alcoholics.

You, in a relationship with an alcoholic, now take on this role. It is *you* who has been the worst offender of this kind of behavior! Look to your past. Who has called in sick for your alcoholic, claiming the actual hangover was the flu? Who has called, time after time, and made excuses or apologies for the alcoholic's behavior of the night before? All of your instincts told you that *you* weren't the one who acted like a jackass, but it is *you* who is sitting by the telephone, ready to make another call of apology to a friend.

Ask yourself who has been making the excuses to the family, yours and the alcoholic's, for missed dates of importance—birthdays, anniversaries, or just a simple telephone call to see how folks are doing? You think, of course, that you have been helping by making all those calls, making all those excuses.

This enabling behavior has been so crippling; it has contributed to your use of the sixth deadly sin, the failure to take risks. The problem is really very simple. Like the other sins of your past we have been looking at, this enabling process ties in with all the others.

Every time your shame, anger, guilt, denial, fear, and non-risk taking all get piled up, you simply perform another enabling act to keep everything in place. The enabling protects the status quo, so none of the other feelings that your old tapes have been playing have to be dealt with. They can just go unanswered as they have been for the time you have been playing them.

A new tape to replace the sin of enabling would be one that says, "No! I'm not going to cover for you any longer! You'll need to face the music on your own!"

Now we both know that has *not* been happening, not by a long shot! You have not been rocking this boat of inaction any more than you rocked any of the others sailing merrily on the seas of your past. Once again, it has been easier for you to pick up the pieces and keep things together than to face the scary changes that will have to be forthcoming if you suddenly stop covering up your alcoholic's behavior.

Like that little child pulling objects off the coffee table, your alcoholic continues to get away with incredible behaviors, behaviors that certainly would not be tolerated if *you* were exhibiting them. How long do you think you could have held your own job with the kinds of excuses that you have worked hard dreaming up to protect your alcoholic when hangover prevents him from showing up on the job?

The kinds of inventiveness that you put into play would drive the Patent Office nuts, they are so unique! I have heard significant others tell of some of the most jim-dandy excuses they were able to present. I once treated one of these people who had been able to use Asian flu as a *written* excuse to her husband's employer, weeks after the well-publicized outbreak had been over.

She got away with this by accompanying the note with a phone call to the personnel office where her alcoholic husband worked, informing them that it was *her* fault for having not taken him to the doctor sooner and that he was just now picking it up after she had had it! Of course she hadn't missed any work because she never had the Asian flu. Neither had he been a victim of that virus. What he had was what is commonly called the "Irish flu," a not-so-kind reference to hangovers caused by drinking!

I'm half Irish and, like the rest of my kin, take the rap for being one of the largest ethnic groups who are alcohol abusers; thus, "Irish flu." Just think of the numbers of times in your past when you have performed similar kinds of skullduggery to enable your alcoholic!

In each of the areas of your past seven deadly sins, you will find circumstances in which the enabling process was the very thing you turned to and, as we learned earlier, was motivated by the fear of risk taking.

When your shame was operating in its full mode, you were particularly anxious to practice enabling so you could protect the alcoholic from embarrassment. Isn't that funny? The alcoholic rarely has any sense of having done anything that is out of line or wrong since the active drinking state sedates inhibitions and the blackout phases conveniently erase most of the shameful episodes from memory.

So *you* practice enabling, in order to cover *the alcoholic's* shame! I refer you to the Bible for one of my favorite examples of this. It is in the first recorded instance of drunkenness: the Book of Genesis, the story of Noah, in verses 20-22 of Chapter 9 we are told:

> Noah was the first tiller of the soil. He planted a vineyard; and he drank of the wine and became drunk, and lay uncovered in his tent. And Ham, the father of Canaan, saw the nakedness of his father, and told his two brothers outside.

Now here comes the enabling part (verse 23):

> Then Shem and Japheth took a garment, laid it upon both their shoulders, and walked backward and *covered the nakedness of their father* [italics mine]; their faces were turned away, and they did not see their father's nakedness.

The two brothers, Shem and Japheth, motivated by their own shame, *prevented* their father, Noah, from realizing the consequences of his drunken behavior. He was going to awaken *covered* instead of having to face the shame of what his drunkenness had done! Thus, they *enabled* him to escape the consequences.

I love it! You see, enabling did not just start with your past behaviors, and that should give you some hope! It also shows us that many times what has been disguised as kindness is really unkind. When your behavior has kept your alcoholic from facing his or her behavior, you are delaying the process of getting well. Your past enabling has nurtured and fostered the disease of alcoholism, instead of throwing a roadblock into the process.

This does not mean that you are responsible for the alcoholism; it only means that your past enabling has put things in that old neutral gear of your lives!

Let's call up the past sin of your anger. Enabling has

definitely come into play here. Because your anger has been buried, and because you always seem to get over it, particularly as the days wear on from the last drinking episode, you have found ways to cover the tracks of the alcoholic.

Suppose you have asked your alcoholic about paying the house mortgage or the apartment rent. He or she has drunk it up or failed to pay it. You are very angry, but other than perhaps a real explosion on your part, which is usually short-lived, you have buried the anger and gone on with your enabling.

The mortgage or the rent has to be paid. Do you force action on the part of your alcoholic? No. It is you on the phone borrowing the money or asking the mortgage company for a short grace period and then making up incredible stories of what tragedy has befallen your alcoholic that made your call necessary.

You are plenty angry, but you have reasoned that, after all, *you* also need a place to live. It has never occurred to you that this process of enabling will just continue to work over and over again. There will be other months, maybe the very next one, when, after you pulled the mortgage or rent payment "out of the fire," you have found yourself facing the exact same situation.

You have gotten just as angry, maybe more so, the next time it happened. But your old tapes of anger allow you to bury it, and you are back on the phone, pleading, begging, or borrowing.

You certainly know how the past sin of your guilt has fostered all kinds of enabling practices. Remember as you read through this book that the differences between enabling and helping are very clear. You always need to ask yourself, "Which is this, enabling or helping?" before you step into a rescue mission for your alcoholic.

In the past, your guilt has opened up new worlds of enabling. You have felt so guilty that you have been willing to do almost anything to wipe away that *mea culpa* and to make things right again. For example, perhaps you have convinced yourself that the alcoholic would not have gotten drunk if you had not invited the Jones couple to bridge, particularly after your companion has told you that he or she doesn't particularly care for them.

Well, you needed another couple to fill out the second table of bridge; the Joneses have always been fun people for you, so they came. He got drunk, and it was your fault for inviting them! The guilt tape starts to roll; you crank up the enabling amplifier to its fullest and, instead of allowing the alcoholic to deal with the real issues of drunkenness, scratch the Joneses from your bridge list.

Then, when it is *another* couple, *another* night, and the alcoholic *still* gets drunk, you are baffled! But your old tape of guilt keeps cranking away, allowing you to feel that you just haven't found the right set of friends, friends who won't upset the alcoholic and cause him to drink and get out of hand.

Rather than confront your alcoholic with the fact that, no matter *who* is invited over, he ends up getting drunk, you just keep on enabling until you probably stop having anyone at all over to play bridge or anything else. Before you know it, you have allowed yourself to become a hermit.

When the old tape of your denial has been playing, your enabling has even encouraged you to continue the mass cover-ups that you have instigated for your alcoholic.

"After all," you have reasoned, "if this isn't really a serious problem, then why shouldn't I help by_____ (insert favorite enabling practice)?" So you blithely go about your merry way, picking up the pieces of destruction that has been wreaked by your alcoholic.

One of the ways this is brought to your attention is by the way you may have enabled your alcoholic to deal or not to deal with her children. Your old tape of denial has played so strongly that you have jumped the kids when there is some little nagging doubt in your mind that it is your alcoholic who was responsible for whatever the fracas was between them.

But you have jumped right in, setting things right, meting out probably unjust punishment, and doing everything you can to avoid facing the problem squarely and taking the risks to make changes. But you can see how it has worked!

The old tape of denial says, "It's not a serious problem; therefore, I need to do whatever needs to be done to smooth things over." All the other old sins then add their choruses to whatever past tape is playing, and you just find more and more reasons to keep on enabling!

It's very obvious that your fear has fostered enabling in your past. You would do anything either to keep people from knowing or to keep the alcoholic from leaving, and you sincerely believe that you will fail in your efforts, so enabling becomes easier than breathing for you and just as involuntary.

You breathe automatically, without thought, and it is the same with your past enabling. You haven't even had to stop and think, "Do I want to enable?" You have just automatically set the enabling amplifier up louder to drive all the old sin tapes even more blaringly into the living rooms of your mind and body.

All of these old sins of your past, then, have allowed the process of enabling, disguised by you as helping. There's practically no element of your daily living with an alcoholic in which you cannot have searched and found many examples of how you have intervened by enabling.

The most pitiful part of all of this, and I have heard it more times than I can relate, is that all of you have so firmly believed that you *had* to do the enabling chores, whatever they were, so that things would get better.

After significant others are in treatment, they begin to see how they have really allowed their enabling to impede the get-well process. They begin to see how the failure to take risks has made enabling the only viable road for them. It is sad how many times we hear a man or woman tearfully choking out, "But I *thought* I was helping!"

Another favorite example of mine, which I used in *Sitting in the Bay Window,* is also worth passing along here. Suppose you are driving along a street and see a person having trouble with a flat tire. You stop and offer to render assistance. The person gratefully accepts your kindness. You get all set up, get out a car jack, and start the tire-changing process. Instead of watching or helping you change the tire, the stranded motorist claims to be "so upset by all this." You suggest the person walk across the street to the convenience store and get a cup of coffee. While the motorist does so, you blithely continue, feeling ever so good about yourself, changing the tire!

The person returns to the repaired car, probably bringing you a nice cup of coffee for your efforts, even offering to pay you for what you have done. You, of course, graciously refuse. You part, feeling *very* good about yourself.

But have you really helped that person? Not really. This motorist still may not know how to change a tire if and when it goes flat again. *You*, the *enabler*, did all the work, instead of inviting the person to stay and watch the procedure that should be followed if such an emergency occurs again.

That person has learned nothing and will undoubtedly find another enabler who will make it unnecessary ever to learn how to make things better for himself or herself. Yes, you helped someone out of a jam, but you also really hindered, or *enabled*.

As you read through and study this book, keep in mind the enabling practices that you have followed in the past, and may be following even today. Not only have they affected your life with an alcoholic, but once enabling has become such a part of your way of living, it becomes a *natural* way of life for you in every aspect. That's scary to me. How does it strike you? Have I pulled on the bell-rope of your memory enough to make you realize that what you thought you were doing to help your alcoholic was, in actuality, impeding or even halting the process of getting well together? I hope so! I hope the bell has gone off loud and clear!

Part II

GETTING HELP—
THE PRESENT

8

What's Out There for Me?

"I don't know what I'd do without my Saturday morning meeting!"

"When I think the whole world's collapsed I remember my group, and things aren't *nearly* as bad."

"It's better than family—do ya know what I mean? My group means more and understands me better than my family!"

These are the kinds of statements that have been made in our Gateway Treatment Center by the dozens and dozens of significant others who have gone through treatment or are in the process of treatment now.

The theme is always pretty much the same: that group support is such an important part of the process of getting well. This accounts for the worldwide acceptance of Al-Anon as a place of inspiration and hope, trust, and care for all those who are living with an alcoholic.

What I want to share with you in this chapter, however, are some other kinds of support, some additional steps that can be taken, either along with Al-Anon groups or in place of them, since no one idea necessarily meets everyone's needs in the same ways. I'm a firm believer in having choices and an equally firm believer in using whatever works to beat the problem!

My own personal belief is that A.A. and/or Al-Anon *in combination with* formal treatment for the disease of alcoholism is the lifelong, best support system there is. Whatever you may choose for help, this chapter is designed to acquaint you with some things you may not be aware of or have not considered, usually because all those past seven deadly sins have gotten in the way.

But here we are in your present, and what we're going to concentrate on are other avenues of getting help, aside from the traditional ways you may now know of or are using. When anyone says to me, "Why fool around with what I'm doing now?" I always tell them that I personally never stop learning about my disease of alcoholism, and every journey into its understanding is a true adventure—something that I can relish and pass on to others.

One of the things that I have been harping on so far is that basically you haven't been doing a whole lot to move forward. You have allowed old tapes of the past to keep you mired down, and now it's time to hook up a new tractor and pull yourself out of the mud puddles of your life.

We have assumed that you are living with or are involved with an actively drinking alcoholic. What you must now consider is that you will need *lifelong help to continue your relationship with a recovering* alcoholic as well. When I wrote *The Joy of Being Sober*, it was subtitled, A Book for Recovering Alcoholics and Those Who Love Them.

The reason for that should be obvious. It is not just the alcoholic who goes into recovery, but also *you*, the significant-other person in his or her life. Whatever joys of sobriety are felt for the alcoholic are also felt, in large measure, by the significantly important person in the alcoholic's life.

In your present state you have been probably just thinking of the alcoholic; that's one of the principal reasons for your lack of risk taking and lack of action to do very much changing. Just surviving has been the big chore! But it's time to come of age now and move into the processes of getting well.

One of the most important tools that can help you explore the best ways for getting help is the *assessment* of the problem. Not all alcoholics are alike; therefore, not all alcoholic relationships and living situations are alike. You need to examine your own particular set of problems and decide what seems to fit best for you.

Therefore, I've prepared a list of questions you should ask yourself as a sort of personal assessment sheet. This is a way for you to come to some honest conclusions about yourself. I use most of these questions and exercises with my own cases in therapy, so I have come to rely on them as being pretty trustworthy.

After we look at these new tools, we'll look at some ways to categorize yourself and therefore narrow down the choices for getting help to those that will tend to meet your own specific needs. First, I'd like you to take a notebook and make two separate columns on a page. Headline each of these columns as follows:

Things I Like About Myself Things I Dislike About Myself

Now list ten items under each column. Be honest! Don't share your list with anyone; this is strictly between us, but mostly it is a self-evaluation tool for you.

You may think that you can easily list ten, twenty, or thirty things you dislike about yourself. A lot of our patients say, "Gee, *that* list is no problem! I just can't think of anything I can list that I like!"

Well, do it my way, no matter how tough it is for you. Limit yourself to ten things you dislike, and ten things you like about yourself. These can be physical things such as "nice figure" or "my height," etc. They can also be personality traits such as "my bad temper" or "I'm nice to people."

You get the idea. Don't put a limit on what categories you use; mix them up if you like. When we look at what you've listed, there will be some real clues as to what is going on with you. Now take your time; don't try to write down the first things that come to your mind.

When you have your lists in opposing columns, under the proper headings, you can get some clues as to what might be going on with you! Suppose your list of likes contains only physical things. What does that tell you about yourself? Does it say, perhaps, "I can only deal with the *way* that I look, and not with how I feel"?

We've already discussed the fact that dealing with your feelings in the past has been pretty scary; maybe you can see, on paper, that it *still* is a scary process. So you've tended to focus on the physical aspects of the very special person that is you. Maybe you have listed only physical things that you dislike about yourself. Does that mean that your emotions are under control? Does it suggest that you believe any personality changes would be too hard to make and therefore are not worthy of listing?

Suppose your list shows more personality items. Perhaps you've written, "I'm always critical of others" or "I have a bad temper." Look at these things closely. Are you being too hard on yourself? Does your list indicate to you that you don't think very much of yourself?

What all this adds up to is a simple tool you can use to analyze your self-esteem. How do *you* feel about *you*? Strictly physical lists of both likes and dislikes always indicate to me that the significant-other person deals only with a "large nose" or "dull, gray eyes," and generally these are things that only plastic surgery or maybe colored contact lenses could correct!

What such a person doesn't want to look at are the things that can be changed through therapy, through self-actualization and self-improvement methods that will help propel them from the fantasy world into the world of reality.

Look at your lists with the idea that it's time to see what you really want to do about making changes in your life. Ask yourself, "Why can I find only three or five things about me that I like, but I could fill a book with what I *don't* like?"

I hear that one a lot! When I do hear it, I refuse to accept the lists until they have been sent back to their creators for more thorough soul-searching.

After you have your lists—remember, you are not sharing them with anyone else—I want you to make a sort of "constellation chart." This is a list of your family background. I use *constellation* because I want you to see that you are the star!

List your parentage and grandparentage, your brothers and sisters, perhaps even very close aunts and uncles, and cousins you feel have had a direct bearing on your life up to this point. And, of course, yourself. Leave a blank line under each name and then note whether the person was alcoholic, had a "drinking problem," or "drank pretty heavily." Also indicate whether the person was a user of prescription medicines like Valium, Librium, and Ativan or of "street drugs" like marijuana, cocaine, amphetamines, and the like.

What are *your* drug uses, if any? Are you an alcohol drinker? List all of these things in the spaces you have provided. When you are finished with this, go back and circle the people who were the major influences on your childhood.

Is there any correlation between, say, a "heavy drinker" and the fact that he or she was your idol in childhood? Are you able to see an emerging pattern in which alcohol/drug abuse has been a significant part of your life?

You might discover, if you didn't already know it, that you are an adult child of an alcoholic. You are, therefore, in need of some specialized understanding and support concerning that issue and how it affects your present state of affairs; namely, your involvement with either an actively drinking or a presently recovering alcoholic.

There is a growing awareness of the adult children of alcoholics, and one of this country's outstanding workers and leaders in that field is Dr. Claudia Black, who was introduced earlier.

If your constellation chart combined with your own suspicions points to the possibility that you're an adult child of an alcoholic, I strongly suggest that you seek a support group made up of others like you.

If you are unsure as to whether there is an adult child support group where you live, go to Al-Anon and ask around. There you'll find many people who have the same problem and either have started such a group and have a trained person to facilitate it or know where such a group exists.

When you're studying your constellation chart, you may find other "stars" in your family, and it will be helpful for you to know what they have done with their alcohol problems, if anything. Are you, perhaps, just perpetuating a long line of do-nothings? It's definitely something for you to think about!

The key to all of this is *honesty* about yourself, your family, your upbringing, your past life, and your present one. If you cheat, it's kind of like solitaire. You can stack the cards to beat the game, but what reward have you gained? Here are some other questions to ask yourself about your own background, which can help you shine a light on what has brought you to the point at which you now find yourself.

1. Has my mother or father hidden a family alcoholic from me?
2. Have I conveniently overlooked the drinking habits of my parents, brothers, or sisters?
3. If I *am* the child of an alcoholic, how is my relationship with my drinking parent now?
4. How is my *own* drinking?
5. Have I become a "drinking buddy" to the alcoholic I'm involved with?
6. *Which* parent, if any, is the drinker?
7. What has anyone else in my family ever done about the problem if it presented itself?
8. Are any other people in my constellation chart in treatment anywhere? Al-Anon? Other support groups?
9. Have I told any others in my chart about *my* problem? What's the reason I haven't? When do I want to do this?
10. How much longer do I need to *protect* others in the chart to avoid getting help for myself?

The more you sit and look at your constellation chart, the more you are going to develop specific questions; believe me! You will be amazed at how you can see patterns in the family developing.

The next step is to determine what role you have

played in the family of your birth. It is almost certain that whatever role—hero, lost child, enabler, family mascot, or any combination of these types—you are *still* carrying on in that role!

Another wonderful resource book for you along these lines is by another outstanding woman, Sharon Wegsheider-Cruse. Sharon's book, *The Family Trap*, will help you define your role and help you see how you have continued to adapt your earlier childhood role to the manner in which you are now living.

If your constellation chart has highlighted your being the adult daughter of an alcoholic father, I would like you to read Linda Leonard's excellent short work, *The Wounded Woman*. In this you can see how healing the relationship between father and daughter can be a mighty influence on how you are acting with your alcoholic relationship now.

You may think I am out to break your budget with these and other titles I will be telling you about, but that's not so. Most of the books are moderately priced by today's standards, and all are available in local libraries, so no excuses!

Let's move on to the disease itself. To gain a good understanding of the alcoholic, what he or she is going through, as well as how the alcoholic arrived at this point, you can read some other books, which represent some of the best literature available today. *Under the Influence, A Guide to the Myths and Realities of Alcoholism*, by James R. Millam and Katherine Ketcham, will give you a detailed description of the physiology of alcoholism.

I would be remiss if I did not refer you to my own *Sitting in the Bay Window, A Book for Parents of Young Alcoholics*, for a detailed description of some of the genetic factors at work in the development of the alcoholic. Another work I give to people who ask for recommendations is Dr. Vernon Johnson's classic, *I'll Quit Tomorrow, Revised*.

A very good friend and colleague, Dr. Gary Forrest, is a prolific author, and his *How to Live with a Problem Drinker and Survive* is highly recommended for even more insight into what you have been allowing yourself to go through.

It is obvious that you should have a copy of the *Big Book of Alcoholics Anonymous*. I believe that the significant-other person, as well as the alcoholic, should read this. Al-Anon books and pamphlets are too numerous to mention here except for two that I particularly like and recommend: *The Dilemma of the Alcoholic Marriage* and *Al-Anon Faces Alcoholism*.

Like all things, the books, questions, and guidelines that I have been sharing with you are tools that can help you find the courage to take some action, to get rid of the old tapes of the past and make some worthwhile, productive changes for the future.

Most times, a *combination* of all these tools and others you will be led to in this book will pave the way to the best roads to recovery for you as an individual who has become caught in the trap of alcoholism.

A patient that I was working with in therapy once told me, "I've always been a stranger to myself!" I like that, because it holds the promise for something exciting to come. What is that excitement? It is discovery! What could be more exciting than learning who you really are? Sure, it's scary! I would never suggest that the things we are going to discuss, like treatment and therapy, are easy. But they *are* some of the passkeys that you will be offered to help you get on with this business of living instead of just *existing* with an alcoholic relationship, whether active or recovering.

Remember, at any step of the way that you begin to compromise honesty, you will find yourself in trouble. Many times I have seen significant-other men and women who have reached the point where they could turn the corner to getting well, only to slide back into a depressive state of inaction because they found an excuse to gloss over certain behaviors.

They compromised their honesty by continuing to enable rather than take the risk of helping in a fashion that was frankly tough, difficult to pursue, yet so necessary if a successful plan was to be put into action.

Nothing that I am suggesting to you should be construed as a bandage for a temporary problem. You are dealing with a life-threatening disease, this alcoholism! If you think that it's going to "go away and leave us alone," you're wrong. Your resolve to begin to replace your old tapes of the past is probably the best first step to your own recovery.

I frankly hope that you are so sick and tired of *being* sick and tired, that you will be chomping at the bit to do something to turn your life around. That's why we ask patients over and over, "What do *you* want to do about it?" We don't *tell* them what to do. It's *you* who has to be willing to do the work! We can't do it for you.

This book is offering you tools to pick up and use. If you do that, the chances are very good that you are going to make some changes for the better in your life. If you let the tools just lie there on the floor, then the chances are equally good that you will remain in a catatonic state of inaction! To use these new tools you must do the following:

- Clearly *understand* your *present* role in the situation.
- *Define* the role that you played in your family, your background, your childhood.
- *Explore* the helping groups of Al-Anon, Adult Children of Alcoholics—whatever model seems to fit with the patterns you have uncovered in your constellation chart.
- *Revise* your lists of likes and dislikes.
- *Discover* the depths of your ego strength, the level of your self-esteem. Be prepared to do something about it and to decide that you cannot continue to live your life in the same fashion that you have been.

It's important to understand that there is one basic misconception you must dispel in your own mind before you can hope to make any progress in your recovery and that of your alcoholic. Whether you've been told this or you earnestly believe it yourself, you have to banish the idea that the problem is the alcoholic's, not yours.

It definitely *is* your problem as well. Make no mistake about that! You have been part of the problem, and now you must be willing to be part of the solution. That's what we are going to discuss in the next chapter.

Your old tapes and thus your old ways are no longer going to fit the new you. Be prepared to catalogue, insert, and *play* the tapes of wellness!

9

Treatment for Both of You

You may think that we are putting the cart before the horse, talking about treatment when you may not even have decided what to do or how to get your alcoholic into treatment. But there is a reason for introducing you to treatment options now. Namely, if I can help arm you with what's waiting out there to provide help for you and your alcoholic, maybe I can help you go on to some risk taking and help you reach for the brass ring of treatment. Let's start with the *kinds* of treatment that are available, and then we'll look at each in detail:

1. long-term hospitalization
2. short-term hospitalization
3. residential
4. short-term outpatient
5. long-term outpatient
6. individual therapy

All of these treatment models are available on a profit, nonprofit, pay-as-you-can (sometimes called *sliding scale*), or public health basis. Let's consider, however, that money should never be used as a reason for not getting into treatment. There is *always* a way to find a program that can help meet your needs. Too often the alcoholic, sly fox that he or she is, can talk you out of treatment on the old saw, "We just can't *afford* it right now!"

Most of the therapists I know can handle that one by getting the alcoholic to agree just to commit the amounts that have been spent on drinking. It's amazing how close that figure will come to a monthly payment for a quality treatment program! Also, do not believe that the programs are not going to try to help you find something you can afford, even if you don't have insurance.

Forward-thinking insurance companies generally will pay 80 to 100 percent for hospitalization of the alcoholic and from 50 to 80 percent for outpatient services. It is unfortunate that certain companies fail to recognize the disease of alcoholism and therefore deny the rights to treatment to their subscribers. What Dark Ages thinking!

Financing of your treatment program is available through the programs themselves and at reasonable or no interest rates. Health professionals want you to get help and will do everything possible to put it within the reach of your budget or to refer you to public or pay-as-you-can programs. OK, that's out of the way, so let's look at each of the programs in more detail.

Long-Term Hospitalization

Well, this pretty much tells you right up front. It means that your alcoholic has been deemed appropriate for a stay in the hospital as a means of treatment. What determines this? Usually an assessment has been made by a professional counselor and/or physician, who takes many factors into consideration.

These people will look at how long the alcoholic has been drinking. Is he drinking right now? How many times, if any, has she been in treatment? Has the alcoholic been able to come off the alcohol without experiencing physical withdrawal symptoms such as hallucinations, delirium tremens, seizures, or just plain shaking, nausea, heavy sweating, and so forth?

An assessment such as this is a complicated process. Too often, you or your alcoholic will make the determination that a particular kind of treatment isn't necessary. You are in no position to judge! Even if you have been through programs of treatment before, without apparent success, that does not mean that treatment would not be successful now.

Alcoholism is a progressive, fatal, and *complicated* disease and must not be taken lightly, particularly during the stages of denial that you have been operating in for so long!

If the intake counselor believes, after taking a short history of the alcoholic's drinking patterns, daily consumption, lengths of withdrawal, withdrawal symptoms, to name a few factors, that hospitalization is proper, then he or she will present a particular plan.

Long-term hospitalization will probably be a twenty-eight or thirty-day maximum hospital stay, with three to five days of that time being used for detoxification. *Detox,* as it is commonly called, is the process whereby the patient is medically controlled over a period of time to "bring him or her down" safely from the withdrawal of the alcohol.

Many people believe that a person cannot be withdrawn "cold turkey" from the drug heroin but *can* be pulled off alcohol without serious problems. This is very wrong! The alcoholic, in advanced stages of the disease, and in the midst of a heavy drinking period, cannot be taken off alcohol without risking the possibility of death by seizure. Thus, detox, to enable the use of nonaddictive sedatives, coupled with drugs to guard against seizures, is used to withdraw the patient safely from alcohol over a period of days.

The number of days a patient will spend in detox will be determined by the medical staff of the facility and will be evaluated on the rate of progress the patient makes in all other areas of the medical withdrawal.

So, we will assume that you and your patient are in a long-term hospital program. You will probably be surprised to find out that your patient will be allowed weekend passes to go home with you after the first seven days of treatment. This helps relieve anxieties and the feeling of being locked up. It also helps the patient reestablish his or her feelings about what it's like to be back home *without* alcohol as a crutch.

During the time your patient is in treatment, you will undoubtedly be involved in the family treatment portion of the program. This can range from group work once a week with a collection of persons like you to sessions with your alcoholic, on a weekly or twice-weekly basis.

Most hospital programs will include education sessions in which you will learn about all aspects of the disease. Depending on the structure of the program, you may attend this with your patient, all of you in one room, or you and the significant other persons will be given sessions as a segregated group. Either way, you *will* learn about this third largest killer of humans!

Short-Term Hospitalization

You may end up in a hospital program that operates for three weeks instead of a full month, so I've called this *short-term*. However, there are even shorter periods of hospital stays, such as detox only. This means that the patient has been assessed as needing help only in coming off the chemical safely; then he or she will be referred to some sort of aftercare, outpatient, or individual care and to A.A. and Al-Anon for follow-up.

Case-specific factors will determine the number of days the patient will spend in the hospital for detox. The medical staff, not you, will determine that. In the meantime, you will probably have no treatment whatsoever. That is, there will not be time or resources to provide you with education sessions or individual or group therapies.

What *will* happen is that you will be talked to by one or more staff people about the necessity for some sort of long-term help for you both. You will be referred to some outpatient programs, to Al-Anon, and quite probably to some individual practitioner. This will give you a wide choice to help you decide what's possible for you in terms of finances and time.

Please keep in mind that there is no way I can be aware of *every* model of treatment that is in place around the country. I am trying to give you a *general* feel for the programs and what they usually offer. Each of the treatment facilities in your area needs to be evaluated by you and your patient as to what seems to suit your needs best. Remember, what's important is that you get *some* kind of help.

Another form of short-term hospitalization might be the open-ended plan. A patient might very well be in a detox ward of a hospital but might need to go past the three to seven days that have been allotted for this process. In this case, your patient might be asked to stay for another few days after getting out of detox, before being transferred or referred to a longer-term outpatient facility.

My gifted partner, Paul Staley, MA, has designed such a program, called Intensicare, which we operate in a cooperative effort between our own Gateway Treatment Center (outpatient, six months) and a Denver inpatient hospital, located currently at the Mercy Medical Center. This unique program combines an intensive ten-day short-term hospitalization program with a five-and-a-half-month outpatient model that is both affordable and heavily family-oriented.

Combinations such as this are possible when health care professionals begin to take harder looks at not only rising costs but *more* and all-encompassing ways to get you and your families into treatment.

Residential

This also is a highly specialized and effective method of treatment that has favorable impact in communities fortunate to have such a facility. In this type of setting a patient is living in a residential-type building or group of buildings, usually for a period of thirty days. It is not a hospital but uses the services of a medical staff to monitor the patients' physical health while they are in treatment.

You will definitely be a part of this kind of treatment model. It will also generally utilize a strong fellowship with A.A. and will use much of the work of A.A. in its program of treatment. Many programs, both full hospital and residential, as well as some outpatient models, will use A.A. and Al-Anon as a part of their treatment model, realizing that this method is an outstanding approach to long-term wellness.

The residential program will accept third-party (insurance) payments, just like a hospital. The main difference is that the patients live in a home setting and are not confined to beds, as in a hospital. You may find that you will be isolated from your alcoholic for a short period of time to give both him or her and the residential staff time to orient toward what work must be done to get well.

When you begin your program of involvement, it can take a few hours to one full day a week, again depending on the model of treatment being used. These settings for residential treatment run a wide range from city-oriented to mountain or oceanside, from desert to isolated.

Residential programs can also be *very* long-term, lasting six months or a year, but these are generally recommended for the patient who is simply unable to function successfully in society for very long periods of time and needs the isolation and intense work that such a long-term program provides.

Your involvement in one of these programs is generally severely limited and may not even be allowed for the first few weeks after the patient enters treatment.

Residential treatment will involve looking forward to the days when you both leave the setting. The staff will be working hard to feed you into an aftercare program of A.A., outpatient, or individual therapy, coupled with Al-Anon, to make sure that you don't slip back into your old tapes.

Almost all programs have some kind of an alumni program that maintains ongoing group support and is a most valuable tool for the recovering alcoholic. You would probably not be involved in such a group unless it were set up from the beginning for significant others to participate.

I have been privileged to work with and participate in such alumni groups through the years, and they were very successful. The outings involved both the patients in recovery and their significant others. There were dances, ice cream "pig-outs," Christmas and New Year's parties galore!

One year our Gateway alumni got together for a Halloween costume party at our center. They took over the entire building, cobwebbed the elevators, staircases, and offices, and completely decorated the place. These well-seeking people danced, popped corn, and played old-fashioned games like apple-bobbing and donut-eating-from-a-string until the wee hours! One look at the panel of photos taken from that party and it's easy to see the impact of what it's like to get well together!

Short-Term Outpatient

This model of treatment can be a very intensive program that lasts several hours a night for a few days or weeks. You might, for example, be involved as a couple for four hours a night, five days a week for two weeks. You might also be in a program that will double that amount of time, and you would take four weeks following this intense schedule.

You would most definitely be a part of such treatment, and it is very likely that the fellowship of A.A. will be utilized as a definite part of the treatment plan. It is a valuable experience, and, again, it will be recommended on the basis of your individual appropriateness for such treatment. A program such as this might very well be affiliated with an inpatient hospital program, and thus there will be a natural flow from one setting to the other.

It does not necessarily mean that your alcoholic would have to be hospitalized first, only that such a program might very well be in place and be recommended by the team making the assessment of your alcoholic.

A short-term outpatient program, like all outpatient programs, is generally less expensive by far than most hospital programs by the very nature of the fact that hospital beds, staff, and services are not required. Generally, the choice of inpatient versus outpatient, whether short-term or long-term, is based on the patient's stage or degree of alcoholism.

If the patient is deemed appropriate to be able to function on the "outside," such as in a job or at school, without any problems with alcohol, then it's very likely that outpatient treatment will be recommended. The ability to function without having to be removed from the environment in which the patient lives, works, and plays is an essential element that is taken into consideration by the assessment team at the time of first contact with the treatment program.

Short-term outpatient care will be structured to allow you to go on from treatment into long-term aftercare of some kind, and any program of this type will be anxious for you to be an active participant from the outset.

Costs are, of course, a factor in this type of treatment, and they will be considered when the individual making the recommendation to you meets with you for an evaluation of treatment for you and the patient.

Bear in mind, once again, that I am giving you *examples* of the various kinds of treatment programs, and with the exception of our own Gateway Treatment Center, which I allude to frequently, I don't expect you to search *specifically* for, say, a one-week or a five-week program. Look instead at what is offered to both you and your patient. Since this is a book for you, my concern is that *you* don't find yourself standing on the outside of treatment, looking in. Remember, you're part of the problem! Be part of the solution!

Long-Term Outpatient

In this type of treatment program, you can expect to spend from three to six months to one year, all on a several-hours-a-week basis. The rationale for long-term outpatient care is to get the family involved and keep them in a treatment model long enough to get old tapes replaced with the wellness tapes that will be necessary for longterm sobriety.

The criteria for admission are the same as for other programs. The key questions are asked just as they are asked in the hospital assessments. Appropriateness for treatment is a major concern; patients who obviously will not maintain sobriety in an outpatient setting are not encouraged to enter that kind of treatment model. They are better off, and so are you, in a hospital program of some type, with the possibility of outpatient *aftercare*.

In a long-term outpatient program you will be given education, individual and group therapy, and family therapy, on a weekly basis. The amount of services you receive, the intensity of the therapy, and all of those other treatment factors will depend on the structure of the program itself.

At our Gateway Treatment Center, the significant other such as yourself receives an *equal* amount of individual and group therapy concentrated work, as does the identified alcoholic patient.

Long-term outpatient care offers the advantage of time to do rather extensive family group work as well, and adolescents and teenagers will find themselves involved in their own groups and education sessions, getting a real handle on the disease and its toll on the family.

Once again, A.A. and Al-Anon may or may not be used as a part of the treatment model in a long-term outpatient setting, depending on the direction of the program. Most outpatient programs will have some kind of working arrangement with physicians or hospitals so that medical needs of their patients can be handled in an appropriate referral manner.

Most outpatient programs that are long-term will probably be operated for profit, but they will be sensitive to helping families find the budgetary means to afford this extensive treatment.

Long-term outpatient treatment has the specific advantage of being able to work rather intensively on many underlying problems of the patients and significant others, problems that surface when the alcohol has been put out of the picture. Specifically, marital problems, family dysfunctions of other types, employment discords, etc., can be examined and given some intensive therapeutic help when there is the time to give it.

Individual Therapy

There is no question in my mind that individual therapy in some form or another is absolutely essential to recovery! You may get it as part of any of the programs that I have outlined for you or on your own from the thousands of qualified, professional therapists and counselors who dedicate their work to helping others learn *how to help themselves*.

Individual therapy is also essential because it enables the alcoholic to deal with all of the factors, physical and psychological, that are contributing to his use of a chemical to live life! The two of you can find practitioners who will see you as a couple or as individuals; there will be no structured treatment program, and this, I think, is the biggest drawback of being limited to individual therapy.

In the next chapter, we are going to discuss this form of treatment in more detail, especially for *you*, but I wanted to make you aware of it as a treatment tool for both of you, if that is the route that is chosen.

So, you can see that there are many doors from which to choose. There are many paths to treatment that you can follow, and the roads will all lead to a better way of life for both of you—for the whole family, if you choose one or more of them to help you.

The fellowship of A.A. and Al-Anon will be your basic tool after treatment and will be available to you wherever you go in your life. Out with the old tapes of inaction!

10

Treatment for You Alone

There might be times when all the pieces just won't or can't come together so that you and your alcoholic can enter treatment together. We could spend a lot of pages discussing what some of those reasons are, but for now, let us assume that for one reason or another you are faced with whether to enter treatment for yourself or not.

There is no question; the debate is closed before it even gets started, as far as I'm concerned! It is absolutely *essential* that you take the bull by the horns and get some real treatment for yourself. If you recall, the statistic is frightening: two out of three females who lose an alcoholic by death or divorce end up hooking themselves back up to another alcoholic, unless they receive some kind of treatment!

What makes this phenomenon occur? I believe it is some kind of "wounded animal" syndrome that is inherent in the significant other. It is some deep, driving force that makes the significant other say, "I didn't *quite* get it right last time; give me another wounded animal to fix! I *know* I can do it *this* time!"

That kind of thinking will lead the helpless significant other—you, to be precise—into one alcoholic relationship after another, each time striving to get a better handle on the problem, and each time making not only the same enabling mistakes, but adding brand-new ones.

So the way out of this "wounded animal" syndrome is to get help for yourself—treatment, in short. What is the difference between the Al-Anon that you may already be involved in and entering some kind of treatment, either private, individual, or programmatic?

Look at Al-Anon as a wonderful bridge between treatment and a life of joy, contentment, and comfort with yourself. Depending on where you get treatment, you will really be learning about alcoholism as a disease. You will learn the hows, whys, and whats of the disease—a basic, working knowledge of what it has been doing to you and how you have been allowing it to work on your life.

You need to have this background. When you have completed treatment, you will undoubtedly be referred to and urged to become part of the fellowship of the millions of men and women in Al-Anon. This is *lifetime* support and it can't be beaten!

Remember that alcoholism is a family disease. Every member of the family has been affected by it. This entire book is devoted to you, a person who has been affected by it, even though you may never touch a drop of John Barleycorn! Thus, it becomes obvious that, if you have been affected by the disease, you also need to be *treated* for the disease, with the same intensity as if you were participating with your alcoholic in a program.

What do I mean by *treatment*, anyhow? Essentially, you should consider treatment a program of education, therapy, and aftercare.

"But," you may say, "I'm *afraid* of therapy!" Well, that's understandable, and nobody's going to chastise you because you express that fear. The Roman historian Livy, who lived from 59 B.C. to A.D. 17, called it like it is. He said, "We fear things in proportion to our ignorance of them." Isn't that about the size of it for you? You fear therapy because you may not know anything about it or have bought some silver-screen distortions of what actually takes place in a therapy session.

Let's look at the two kinds of therapy that you will probably become involved with alone.

Individual Treatment

The first, and perhaps most fearful to you, is the sessions that are individual—just you and your therapist, alone in a private room, working together on your problems. Now don't confuse a therapy session with an analysis session or even with a psychiatric session. The two are different from what you will experience.

A therapist dealing with chemical dependency is fully aware of how you have been affected by the disease. He or she is interested in your doing the work of getting well and will want you to proceed at your own rate of speed. Therapy for you will by and large center on your feelings about certain actions that you have taken or failed to take and what you want to do to make changes.

My patients are frustrated when I say, "Well, Ruthie, what do *you* want to do about that?" as opposed to "Ruthie, here's what I think you *should* do about that!"

Therapists group themselves into classifications of styles of conducting therapy. It's good for you to know what some of these styles are, even though you will probably not know what particular manner your assigned or selected therapist practices until after you are more familiar with the sessions.

A client-centered therapist is pretty laid back, focusing almost exclusively on you and your feelings, making you work very hard to admit the particular feelings that you have been experiencing.

Some, as in the way I practice, tend to be more direct, more confrontational. It doesn't make us very popular at times, but when used in the proper fashion, it can be very effective.

Other therapists are reality-oriented, based on the work of Dr. William Glasser, who instructed his patients that they would be treated as "interested in getting well" *if* they were acting in a responsible manner. Acting *irresponsibly* indicated to Dr. Glasser that the patient was still in a state of sickness and thus would be treated that way. Reality therapy emphasizes moral values and does not concern itself with the patient's past, choosing to concentrate instead on the present and the future.

Glasser believes that the therapist faces the task of teaching his or her patients to "acquire the ability to fulfill their needs and to do so in a way that does not deprive others of the ability to fulfill their needs."

I like that, and I use these methods a lot in dealing with significant others. This may be one of the methods that will be used by the therapist you select. There's nothing very scary about any of this; you probably won't do any lying down on an analytic couch, à la Freud, nor will you be put in any hypnotic trances or otherwise chemically induced with "truth serum" or any other hocus-pocus stuff you may have read about or seen in sci-fi at the local cinema!

Now, are you disappointed? I hope not, for individual therapy is a challenging and most rewarding method for you to begin to look at the ways in which you have been doing things and then discover new and better tools to use to strengthen your individual life.

If you were my patient, I would be telling you that I will simply try to hold a mirror up to you and allow you to see your own behavioral reflections. Your therapist will help you recognize your behavior for what it is, using all of the old tapes that you never knew you played, and then will help you replace them with new tapes.

Therapy is a very *healthy* process, and you will soon look forward to your individual sessions as a method to allow you to delve into your "garbage bag" and get rid of what has been choking you for years! Doesn't the prospect of being able to dump all that old stuff sound good to you? It should!

You have been running around in circles, repeating the same old mistakes over and over, thus contributing to the set of statistics I gave you earlier, becoming one of those who will repeat a relationship with another wounded animal time after time!

Individual therapy will help you explore your past, true, but will not necessarily *dwell* on it, relying instead on the awareness of what you have done or not done previously and then helping you see the better alternate roads that can be traveled in your future. All of the elements that we have been looking at together in this book come into play in your individual therapy sessions. You will gain the power to look at the seven deadly sins of your past to see how they have controlled your every thought and action concerning your alcoholic, and to learn how to make changes.

The key is that you will make the decisions for or against change, based on the amount of work that you are willing to do. If individual therapy is scary to you, it may be because you are afraid of hard work.

"Is therapy a sort of *confession* process?" one woman asked me during an initial interview session. My answer was, "Sure, with some major differences, however. I'm not a priest who will offer any kind of penance, nor do I have the authority to grant any kind of forgiveness or absolution."

But it is a known fact that those who confide in others seem to have fewer health problems than those who have been burying their feelings all their lives. Psychologist James Pennebaker of Southern Methodist University was recently quoted in *Prevention* magazine: "The strain of not confiding emotional burdens of any kind creates a great psychological stress. . . . Not surprisingly, nonconfiders had more stress-related health problems." Pennebaker also concluded, "They also had more everyday ills, too, like colds and flu."

Dr. Pennebaker, along with his colleague at SMU, Robin O'Heeron, believes that "therapists, rabbis, or ministers are good to talk to because they are trained to be supportive and nonjudgmental." Pennebaker believes, along with the rest of us in this field, I'm sure, that "it's never too late to unload."

So the individual therapy process gives you the chance to unload the heavy burden that has been on your shoulders, the burden of feeling responsible for the alcoholic and the life that he or she has destined for the two of you.

Group Therapy

Another process of therapy that will be opened to you is group therapy. As the name implies, you and several others of your predicament will meet on a regular basis and go through the process of sharing experiences, hurts, and solutions to problems that you all face as a group of significant others.

Don't think you can sit in a small group and talk? Don't, then! Sit and *listen* for a while, until your comfort zone has been approached, and then perhaps you can share an incident or two that is bound to help someone else who is struggling with the same problem. After all, you are in treatment to *get* well and to *stay* well, and you have not been able to do it alone. Group therapy allows you the opportunity to use the power, the strength of the group, to explore better ways to do things, clearer ways of thinking about things, and *newer* tapes to play!

Your group therapy sessions may be on a daily, weekly, or even monthly basis. They (such as Al-Anon) could involve several groups in a single day/night period. Approach whatever program is best suited to your schedule, but remember that you have nothing to fear from group therapy.

Whatever you may have heard, the awkwardness of such a first-time experience will quickly disappear as you feel the skills of the trained facilitator (therapist, counselor, etc.) take command of the group process and begin to move it off dead center.

You will become aware of this group power I alluded to earlier. It is a special kind of bonding that you will begin to feel, one for another, and will perhaps become one of the most moving experiences of your life. I tell each new group of either recovering persons or significant others that start into treatment that they will probably never feel such close intimacy with any one group of people as they will feel for each other before treatment ends.

It will surpass the experiences of fraternity or sorority life, church and Sunday school and temple, because the group deals with such personal and intimate emotions that you have believed they were exclusively yours.

Thus, the experience of this special group will begin to work wonders. You will begin to care about other group members, noticing their absences or their ill health. You will find yourself relating to others in a way that you always hoped would be yours but that somehow managed to elude you.

I have seen significant others plow their way through heavy snowstorms to make group! Many a one of you has left a sickbed to get dressed and to group because you needed the help, love, and support that you have found there. When you finally cross the bridge from treatment to Al-Anon or other aftercare, you will already have learned this valuable bonding process, and you will respect its power and its demands. The group can be a jealous mistress, indeed!

The process of education that treatment for you alone provides is of great value. You need to *know* about the disease, where it came from in your alcoholic, where and how it is growing, and how it can be put into remission for life. Treatment programs specialize in this process of education, utilizing the faculty of the program to present lectures, films, videotapes, and recorded material as well as printed material about this disease.

Through the educational process you will begin to understand the dynamics of the disease and, most important, the part that you have unwittingly (sometimes *fully aware*) played in the progression of the disease in the alcoholic man or woman with whom you are involved. Even if your alcoholic has not entered treatment with you, it becomes *imperative* that you get this education.

Permit me to let you ask why just this once. Because, if you do not *learn* about the disease, its causes, and its by-products, both emotional and physical, you will go out and repeat the same mistakes over and over again!

Talk about scary! Now *that's* scary! So for you and all significant others, education about the disease begins to *free* you from the bondage in which you have allowed yourself to become a slave. Knowledge will set you on a course of personal freedom, not necessarily from the alcoholic of your current life, but from the sureness of making the *same* mistake again.

You are going to be exposed in treatment education to all phases of the disease that have combined to produce this alcoholic. You will get the opportunity to peel off layers and layers of guilt and responsibility as you learn that you really had nothing to do with it after all, but have merely been *allowing* yourself to feel the immense responsibility, which has been carefully orchestrated by your alcoholic.

Treatment will not be a fast process for you, nor should it be. You have spent a very long time being sick, so it only stands to reason that it's going to take some hard time to get well. Most of you would like things to get better overnight, but then that's the nature of human beings, imperfect and impatient creatures that we are.

For most of you, as soon as you enter treatment, the healing process will begin. That's why the delays that you may allow to happen only hurt you in the long run. What is the reason that you delay getting help for yourself? It is the same set of reasons that has caused you not to take any action with *any* of these problems of your alcoholic life. It calls for daring—for risk taking.

By now, we know that you have not exactly won any gold medals for taking risks. But you can change all that! Go ahead and get out the Yellow Pages and look under "Alcoholism Information and Treatment Centers."

There will be a number of places, programs, and people from which to choose. Alcoholics Anonymous will help refer you to treatment in addition to helping you find an Al-Anon program that could start you off.

Are you short of funds? Are funds perhaps nonexistent? Your local mental health association is funded to provide you with individual counseling as well as to help you get group support. You may find these programs unable to supply the much-needed full-scale education program that a private treatment center will offer, but then you never know until you check it out!

Some programs will refer you from the very start to one of their staff of consultants who can and will see you on an individual fee-for-services basis. Others will want you to be in the full program, taking part in all of its elements, just as if you had your alcoholic in treatment with you. The important things to remember are these:

1. Seek treatment help for yourself to prevent you from making the same mistakes over and over.

2. Find a treatment program that makes you comfortable with the process of getting well. You will know after spending some time at the initial intake session whether or not this program is for you.
3. Don't set impossible restrictions for the times that you can be available for therapy and for the important group and education sessions. You need to make *some* effort here!
4. Make others around you—boss, family and friends— aware that you are seeking help and will need some cooperation from them, such as extra time off or babysitting, to help you participate in treatment.

Finally, it is *imperative* that you test the curiosity of your alcoholic about your treatment program. He or she is going to feel threatened and may even be more hostile than usual, making fun of you because you are getting help. You will just hear louder than ever that it is *you* who is the sick one and that he or she has finally been proven right since you are in treatment!

It's OK! Just take the barbs. You might find that the alcoholic gets more curious about "what the hell goes on down there," referring to your treatment center visits. That's the kind of thing that you want to happen! Get the fish testing the bait and then sock it to 'em!

As we continue, you and I, we'll look at specific ways, such as the intervention, to get your alcoholic help when he or she doesn't really want it. For now, concentrate on what you have just read. Think long and hard about how many times you have repeated your mistakes in dealing with the alcoholic. Think of how many times you have vowed "never again," only to find yourself right back in the soup, doing all the enabling, excuse making, lying, and guilt building that has been a pattern of your life.

Be honest with yourself. Take a long, careful look at yourself in the mirror. Isn't it time you got help for yourself? Aren't you really sick and tired of *being* sick and tired?

11

Going On: The Aftercare Experience

"I'm *tired* of giving up all my spare time."

"God! Is there no end to this?"

"How much *more* am I expected to do?"

That's you talking, hoping *someone* is out there listening to your complaints about the amount of time and the number of days and nights that you and your hopefully now recovering alcoholic have been devoting to treatment.

It seems as if the particular program that you have selected is coming to its scheduled end, and you have begun to hear the staff of therapists or program people talk to you about aftercare. What is it, anyhow, and what makes it important?

As the term clearly implies, it is the *continuing* care that is offered on a long-term basis, *after* the formal part of your treatment program is completed. You have attended all the educational lectures on the disease of alcoholism and hopefully have been able to pick up one or two of them the second time they were offered in the sequence.

You have been in some sort of structured group therapy, and hopefully you have been given individual therapy as well, so that you have a pretty good handle on what this disease is all about and what effects it has had on you both. You are anxious to get on with your life, and the thought of giving even *more* time to treatment is, to say the least, depressing!

But aftercare is a *vital* part of the linking chains of sobriety as you and your alcoholic forge through your lives together. It is aftercare that will always be the link you can count on for continuing support, and that's why we are going to look at some aspects of this part of your treatment.

In my professional opinion, there is nothing better for *lifetime* care for you and the millions of other alcoholics and their significant others than the fellowship of Alcoholics Anonymous! Wherever you go in the world, you will be able to find a meeting. A.A. has service centers located in almost every major city in the United States. In addition, you can generally find an A.A. telephone number listed on the first page of your local telephone directory.

As I said earlier in this book, it is my belief that A.A., *in combination with treatment,* is the ideal way to tackle and keep this disease in remission. Making the transition from formal treatment to A.A. is helpful if you have someone, a sponsor perhaps, who will begin taking you to meetings that are just right for you. Many treatment programs will begin to feed you into selected A.A. groups as you are nearing the end of your treatment program. Others will have used the A.A. program as a regular part of their treatment plan, and thus you will already have some experience with the fellowship.

Other kinds of aftercare will focus on your needs to remain in *formalized* therapy, such as individual or marital counseling. The absence of the alcohol in your lives has very surely opened up that Pandora's box of other difficulties that exist in your relationship, and it may be advisable to continue to work on those problems with the aid of a skilled professional.

Mind you, the problems have probably *always* been there, but the alcohol was masking them, and all you were focusing on was getting the drinking out of the way. Now that that chore hopefully has been accomplished, you, the significant other, can painfully see that the drinking wasn't the *only* problem in the relationship!

I call particular attention to *your* being the one to come to this awareness because the alcoholic so often believes that the drinking was the only thing wrong with the relationship. What a surprise for him or her to learn that there are still difficulties, that there *have been* difficulties, and that they need to be worked on by two clear-headed people!

So often I hear the alcoholic say in a group session or a conjoint (two of you alone with the therapist) session, "I *quit* drinking! What *more* do you want?"

What *more*, indeed? You would like to get back the things that made the relationship exciting to begin with, and while I believe you should concentrate on going on with your life instead of trying to recapture what was, you will very probably need the skills of a therapist to help you.

Aftercare couple's groups, where a therapist or facilitator is available, is another way to cross the bridge from treatment to aftercare—to *ongoing* care! These groups are generally the outcropping of a treatment program's structure. You have completed the formal program for the designated time that was set aside, and now you are given the opportunity to continue into these specialized kinds of groups.

In private, profit-oriented treatment programs, these groups have a minimal charge. They usually pay only for the services of the therapist or group facilitator. You may even find certain kinds of aftercare packages that will offer couple's group sessions on a weekly basis and perhaps one or two conjoint therapy sessions a month.

Either way, the decision will always be up to you and your partner in treatment. You may feel you are getting burned out on therapy. You may have the very real thought that you'll never be able to do this sobriety thing alone, or at least without professional help, for the rest of your life!

In some cases, that may be exactly right. But in most cases, you will begin to know when you are getting it right and find yourselves using the tools of wellness to *keep* yourselves well. This doesn't always come about, however, at the most convenient time; that is, when you are finishing the formal treatment program and you find yourself wanting more. That's why treatment centers and programs offer such continuing care options.

You can get a pretty good feel for the particular state you are in as you listen to how your partner is responding to questions raised at group or conjoint therapy sessions.

What does your *instinct* tell you about the way you feel as you are leaving your treatment? Are you ready to leave? Do you feel confident?

Here is a list of questions to ask yourself when you are nearing the end of treatment. It's a checklist to help you make decisions about formal aftercare. Remember, whatever you decide, the use of your A.A. program, coupled with whatever formal aftercare program you may choose, is a real insurance policy.

1. Am I feeling as if I know all or most of the answers to questions the rest of the group is asking?
2. How has my *comfort* level been lately? Am I cranky or irritable with others?
3. Do I feel insecure with leaving the safety of this group? of this place? of our (my) therapist?
4. Have I found myself being *resentful* of my alcoholic?
5. Have I been *afraid* to go out to social occasions?
6. Do I still feel *responsible* for my alcoholic?
7. Am I still *avoiding* talking about our problems as a couple?
8. Are certain things like sex still *taboo* for discussion, either in group or in our marital sessions?
9. Am I acting like I was at the beginning of treatment? Do I feel like I'm letting my emotions run my mouth?
10. Do I honestly believe that we are *ready* to leave treatment and that we know the danger signs of a relapse?

This is just a brief list to test your security with leaving a formal treatment program. If you found that this checklist raised more questions in your mind, if you have a sense of being unsure, then the chances are you may need to stay in some sort of *structured* aftercare for a little longer.

There is such a tendency to let down after finishing a rigorous program of treatment that it will be easy for you to agree to chuck it, to leave treatment and not make any

efforts whatsoever to keep working. It's a shame if you let
that happen, because when you leave the formal treatment you are really ready to *start* on the lifelong process of
staying well together. There are many ways that you can
keep working at this business of staying well.

Often, I see couples who have completed treatment
on a "tune-up" basis. This got started with me years ago
when a young couple called and said they had just gotten
their car overhauled, were in the process of repainting
their house for summer, and had found themselves starting old habits of noncommunication.

"Jack," Dave said, "I think Patty and I need a spring
tune-up!"

We have laughed about that for years, and sure enough,
I still do "spring tune-ups" for couples as a part of their
continuing aftercare. We do a few conjoint sessions, say
three or four, usually revolving around specific issues that
the couple has been unable to resolve. Then, with the
couple feeling good about themselves, resharpening their
tools of communication and concern, we send them off
until another tune-up time, if needed.

In the next chapter, you and I will look at a specific
plan for these tune-ups and how they can be of benefit to
you, whether you use a professional or do them yourself.

An important element to be considered by both of
you will be the expense involved in going on with some
aftercare. Fortunately, cost is no factor in the fellowship of
A.A., since it's free! There are really no excuses for not
staying involved somewhere, if you are still feeling shaky
about leaving.

You may not find an open couple's group in the A.A.
in your town. But why not *start* one? Not long ago, I was
invited to spend part of my Sunday evening with four
couples who had completed treatment in our program
many months ago. They meet every Sunday in one another's houses as a home group.

For the first hour, the significant others meet in one
part of the house, while the recovering folks meet in
another. For the second hour, they come together as
couples and work a one-hour session without a facilitator.

They spend the rest of their evening with Trivial Pursuit, bridge, videos, football games, or what have you.

When they got bogged down on a sensitive issue, they called and asked me if I would come and help them unsnarl the problem. It was a wonderful experience and did me a world of good to see our graduates working so hard on their own in a really strong aftercare program!

So, alumni can get together as an aftercare plan, and that's something else that won't cost you anything except the effort to go. If you feel that you need continuing individual work, don't hesitate to get it!

You can see the individual therapist you have been working with on a fairly regular basis, gradually tapering off your visits as you supplement them with Al-Anon and other forms of support.

When a group of our female patients were completing their program of treatment, they determined that they didn't want to lose contact with each other. They came to us, and we endorsed their plan to keep meeting together as recovering females, using our facility, on Saturdays.

This group, now calling themselves Sisters in Sobriety (SIS for short), is picking up several new attendees a month and is working very hard at maintaining sobriety! It's a wonderful testimony to their desire to create their own aftercare and shows that there are very few limits to what can be done, if you really want to do it.

In recovery, there really is no end, as such. Since the disease of alcoholism is not curable, you are constantly going to be living with it. That means that there is no logical *conclusion* to the care you need to give yourself. The more confident that you feel you are getting, the more trouble you may be heading for! You have been learning how the old tapes of your past have been so influential in your life. They can come back at any time that you let down and feel cocky, and they will knock you quickly off your high horse.

In *The Joy of Being Sober*, I introduced readers to the "mouse turds" of life; these are the little piddly things that seem to get in the way of recovery. You know what I mean: the inconsequential, minor irritation of everyday living. The recovering alcoholic can easily let these little things become major stumbling blocks to getting well.

As well as you may think you are, you can find yourself suddenly tripping and falling over these little "mouse turds" yourself, both as an individual and as a couple in recovery. Aftercare is effective in keeping you focused on the really important aspects of your life and not constantly picking yourself up off the floor of life where you have fallen!

In aftercare, a rigid structure isn't necessary. What's important is for you to get a feel for what's best for you, for what seems to *work* to keep your lives going in a growing and healthful fashion. Many significant others find they miss the formal structure of group or of conjoint therapy with a therapist to help them over the rough spots.

Others, feeling confident about the tools they have learned, are perfectly happy to get involved in home groups of A.A., Al-Anon, or other couple's support programming. I think the thing that is most dangerous, however, is to wait until your recovery has already started to rupture. If you have waited until this damage is under way, then you may find the work harder in coming back into aftercare as a treatment tool. What you may need is the following recovery checklist to see how you may be coming along with your life after treatment has been completed.

There is no set time limit on when you may need to use this checklist, but if *any* of these symptoms show up, look at all the others on the list and see how you are stacking up.

Recovery Checklist

1. Am I finding myself being more irritable lately?
2. Do I seem to want everything to happen faster?
3. Have I noticed that my alcoholic isn't really interested in working on our relationship?
4. Do I find myself getting moodier lately?
5. Am I "walking on eggshells"? Do I feel as if the

next thing I say to my alcoholic is going to be the start of another argument?

6. Have I been hesitant to share my *feelings* with my alcoholic?

7. Do I sometimes wish that the alcoholic *hadn't* stopped drinking?

8. Have I been confronting *others,* but not my alcoholic, lately? Am I making someone else pay for what we're going through?

9. Am I finding excuses to be too busy for A.A., Al-Anon, or support group meetings?

10. Have I been doing *weird* things lately, like cleaning my house at one or two in the morning?

These are some of the behaviors that can cause you to ask whether it is time for some *structured* aftercare. Something isn't going right for you in recovery, either as an individual or as a couple, and these early warning signs can be your signal to get into action.

Some of the things on this list indicate you are just now feeling the *anger* at being involved with an alcoholic, even though your alcoholic has stopped drinking and is in the recovery process. But you have been holding things in for so long that they have just now begun to seep out of you, and you are finding yourself going through many kinds of *compulsive* behaviors, such as the wee-hours housecleaning bit.

This is a way your emotions tell you that you are not yet as well as you may have thought, that there is still a lot of work for you to do, and that you'd better heed the warning signs! When every time you want to say something you hesitate, or fail to speak your mind for fear of having another Mount St. Helens eruption go off in your living room, then aftercare is beckoning you, loud and strong! Don't fail to heed the siren's call!

12

Tuning Up Your Relationship

If you have bought a car recently, or are still nursing the old buggy along on a month-to-month basis, you are very aware of the need for periodic tune-ups. It's no different in your relationship with a recovering alcoholic. You see, your relationship is *totally* different in sobriety from when you were living with an actively drinking alcoholic.

It stands to reason, therefore, that you will need to tune up your relationship, to look under the hood, change the emotional oil, and replace the poorly functioning spark plugs! The fact that *both* of you have been affected by this alcoholism is an even better reason for *both* of you to want to get a relationship tune-up. It isn't a question of just one of you going out and getting better and leaving the other person at home to fend for himself!

That old bugaboo, communications, is generally where most recovering couples bog down, unable to progress. They just continue to wonder to themselves, "What's wrong here?"

When we talk of the ability to communicate we are talking about having *two* parts of an equation. Most of us are pretty good at one part, that of being the sender of messages. What we are missing is the part of the equation that is equally important: that of being a receiver of messages. Being a good listener means that you hear what is being said and that you interpret the messages based on what you actually hear and not on what you *thought* you heard.

When two recovering people, the significant other and the recovering alcoholic, sit down in the car or the living room or bedroom and begin to talk, what actually happens? When the alcohol was in the picture, most such conversations consisted of the alcoholic spending two hours or more telling *you* what was wrong with *you*, instead of ever examining the drinking and what it was doing to the relationship. Does that sound familiar?

Well, now you have a different set of circumstances, one that calls for two good sets of communicating elements: a good sender and a good receiver. When, in sobriety, you are beginning to feel that you are neither listening nor receiving clear and concise messages, it's probably time for a tune-up.

Where do you go for this? I suggest you head right back to the treatment module from which you came: either a private therapist, or the program that was working with you and the staff with which you have become most familiar.

The comfort level of treatment is very important. You are not going to accomplish a whole lot if you and your alcoholic are still fighting the program and, hence, fighting the tools that can be set before you to help you get well.

I want to emphasize again the importance of your understanding that all you are given in treatment is a set of tools to use in your own programs of recovery. No one can do it for you.

Our patients all hear the message loud and clear: "It's up to *you* whether you get well! If you pick up the tools and *use* them, you have a pretty good chance. If you just let them lie there on the floor, you'll probably stay sick!" We go on to state emphatically, "If you *do* get well, it'll be *you* who wears the gold medal! If you stay *sick*, it'll also be *you* who wears the crown of thorns!"

This is my method of making sure the individual or the couple completely understands that, as a therapist, I don't have any power to make them well. Only *they* have the power to pick up the tools that I will gladly hand them and to give themselves a chance at wellness.

When you and your recovering person are mincing

around the house, avoiding each other, yet knowing that you both need to talk, what do you do about it? Probably not much. It's too scary, just as a lot of the recovering process is and as most of your past seven deadly sins were.

But before you call for a tune-up session, you can use a few tools to help you make some progress on your own. For one, you can use the tool of the ten-minute drill that I wrote about in *The Joy of Being Sober*.

To summarize that tool, you and your alcoholic decide to talk together for ten minutes without *any* interruptions of TV, radio, stereo, kids (very important), pets (they become "third parties"), and telephones or door bells!

Set the timer on your kitchen range for ten minutes; use the clock radio with its annoying buzzer; use *anything* that will notify you when ten minutes have elapsed. Then sit down and *talk* and *listen* to each other!

It will be important talk—not the common garden variety "How was your day?" but gut-level-feelings talk. You get into this by using "I" statements that express how *you* feel. For example: "I *feel* as if we are both walking on eggshells, Michael. Can you help me figure out why I'm feeling like this?"

Now this is a direct *request* on your part to receive help with your feelings, and it cannot in any way be mistaken as a criticism of what "Michael" is or is not doing. It is a very effective way to open your own ten-minute drill.

When the buzzer goes off, you both have the right and the option to test each other's feelings about going on for another ten-minute segment or quitting because anger or some other emotion has gotten in the way and is preventing you from being an active sender or receiver in the drill.

If the ten-minute drills don't seem to work, you can ask yourselves the "trigger" question; namely, "What's going on with us that seems to make it impossible to talk for even ten minutes?"

You'll quickly decide that a tune-up with your professional is called for. You need someone to unstick the gears from neutral and get you moving again.

Another tool that can be used before you call for a tune-up with a professional is the "let's try writing" tool. Here, actually sitting down to talk and listen about your feelings is so awkward, now that you don't have a therapist to help you, that you are going to have to resort to another method. That method is simply to write a *feelings* letter. You are all aware of the trick that your childhood might have spawned when your anger got out of hand at someone and you sat down and wrote a "hate note." Lots of times, you never even sent this note, but just putting it on paper really helped you get rid of the anger that you were feeling but were unable to express.

The same thing can work with the two of you. If the face-to-face conversations imposed by a ten-minute drill are not working, then you can both agree to jot down your feelings. I suggest to patients that they write down exactly how they feel, in letter form, and then *wait* three days.

At the end of this self-imposed time period, you reread the letter, make whatever changes you so desire, then *mail* the letter to your alcoholic. Don't send it to the abuser's office; send it to the home where you both live. Sure, it's going to cost you a stamp, but it's going to get the attention of the receiver.

In this letter you can say the things that you have not been able to say in the face-to-face sessions of the ten-minute drill. He or she can respond verbally if desired but should do so *only* in the safety of the rules of the ten-minute drill. If that isn't successful, you can suggest that a tune-up with your professional seems to be in order so that the communications logjam can be broken.

When the couples who are in treatment with us sit across the room from each other, several months into their sobriety, they all invariably say that their communications still are the biggest hang-up they are experiencing. Many of them freely admit that, when they were drinking, this didn't seem to be a problem at all.

When these people are confronted about that, they admit that they didn't do a lot of serious communicating; they talked about only superficial kinds of things. Serious matters were too threatening to their relationship, so they buried them with more alcohol on the part of the drinker and more burying of feeling on the part of the significant other.

As we have learned, then, when the alcohol is out of the way, these untended feelings come rising to the surface, demanding to be heard and hopefully to be counted, rather than discounted, through some positive actions. Discounting those feelings is evidenced when one of you is finding it easier to express his or her feelings, but the partner is saying, "I don't give a damn *how* you feel!" That will surely call for a tune-up to help you understand the reasons behind such a statement.

The tune-up is a wonderful time for you to get a reading on how you are fitting in with others, how you are melding as a sober couple with those around you who may still be drinking and with whom you are still feeling uncomfortable. Suppose you have been turning down all kinds of invitations to do things with other people. What's this all about, anyhow? Surely you don't want to turn into a couple of hermit crabs, do you? Of course not!

Well, if it has become a habit to say no to your friends, a tune-up is in order.

Your therapist can help find a couple's group for you, maybe even a different one from the home group you started out with. More important, though, is the fact that the therapist will help you *confront* the fear that is making you refuse invitations from your friends. That's probably the thing that has kept you at home in the security of your own four walls—*fear*.

"My God!" you gasp. "They might be serving *booze* at their bridge party!" Well, yes, they might! And you are *afraid* to go because of it. Well, a tune-up might be just the thing to make you pick up those tools that you laid down now that you're out of treatment and use them again. It is in the atmosphere of the therapist's office that you will quickly regain the methods that you have put aside for dealing with life and the drinking society in which we all live.

I surely don't mean to imply here that you have to go back and enter full treatment. You may not even have to spend one more dime in treatment if you will make the effort to take your tune-up to your A.A. or Al-Anon meeting. Maybe you have put off having or ever getting an AA sponsor. Re-examine that possibility. Finding someone who is going or has gone through exactly what you are now experiencing is a very real step forward, and that person will help get you back on track.

One of the best ways I know for determining whether a tune-up might be in order is to ask yourself, "Am I *happier* now than when the alcoholic was drinking?" If the answer is "No," or "I'm not sure," then you need a tune-up. Anyone who would go back to the hellish life of the past has definitely stumbled over so many of those "mouse turds" that he or she can't walk straight anymore. A tune-up can get you back on the right path.

The thing about your tune-up is that it's a *temporary* measure to help clarify feelings and issues that you two have not been able to do for yourselves. But it *does* have an end! You can definitely know that you might need or want only one or two sessions with your professional to unsnarl the basic feelings, and then you can re-enter the A.A., Al-Anon, or couple's groups that you have been avoiding.

There will be those that will tell you that you don't need to spend any more money on treatment, but I have found from experience that at least one professional session with your therapist is money well spent. He or she can quickly get to the emotional logjam that you are in, and then you can begin to start the stream of conversations flowing again.

Groups are not as good at this as is the conjoint technique we have discussed. Groups too often have a tendency not to be able to see what is *causing* the problem, but to focus on *what* the problem is. If you can't determine the reason for a problem, it will continue to crop up, and you will continue just to deal with the surface issues, instead of the root cause.

It's very much like a toothache. If you just continue to take aspirin for the pain, and never get to the dentist to see what's *causing* the pain, then the condition will persist. You might be successful in temporarily easing the discomfort, but long-term relief will come only when the root cause is discovered and treated.

It's the same thing with your relationship and any of the problems that your recovering alcoholic may have allowed to come to the surface. If you aren't willing to get at the root of what's causing the problems, they will continue to be issues between you.

The tune-up, like other tools we have been discussing, is a proven method of helping you through trying times. It is also a safe place for you to work on problems. The same kinds of atmosphere that persisted when you were in treatment are waiting there for you, if you return for an aftercare tune-up.

Earlier, when we were looking at the ten-minute drill, I mentioned not having kids or pets around when you're trying to talk. That bears further explanation and is another reason for using the tune-up to ensure the kinds of concentration that are necessary for you to get down to business and do some good hard work.

Kids will automatically demand your attention, and they often are jealous of seeing the two of you just trying to have time by yourselves. It makes them nervous when they see you having a serious discussion because it often reminds them of the kinds of things they witnessed when there was active drinking going on; it wasn't very pleasant.

Pets are equally disturbing. I mentioned they often become third parties to your conversations and only cause a further block. You know what I mean. It goes something like this:

> HE (rubbing the dog's ears): So, Malcolm, "Mommy" thinks I'm spending too much money on stereo gear, huh?
>
> SHE (speaking to Malcolm): Now, Malcolm, that *isn't* what I said! "Daddy" just isn't listening to me!
>
> HE (still talking to Malcolm): *You* tell "Mommy" that I think she doesn't want me to buy *anything* for myself!

*   *   *

Poor Malcolm! He's taking the rap for being the family dog! He got himself right into a third-party position in the midst of this discussion, and both "Mommy" and "Daddy" are talking *through* him!

You see, it becomes easier for couples to communicate through a third party when the confrontation of one another directly involves taking too much risk! The couple that speaks through their pets definitely needs to replace the "Malcolms" of their life with their therapist, who can help them relearn the process of speaking to one another in a direct, concise, two-party conversation!

For any progress to be made, you must be open to suggestion. You must realize that there is no magic formula for getting well and that, for every person, the amount of time spent in therapy, in *structured* help, is different. Don't be discouraged if you feel that you are the only ones who need a tune-up. It's certainly no shame that you may not have gotten everything down pat the first time.

The tune-up can be a very rewarding experience for you even for the first several *years* of sobriety. It's like a bank account: the more you put into it, the more it grows.

I have worked with couples who budget a regular amount for their yearly tune-up, a session or two they use just before they go on vacation. It helps them put their lives into perspective and go over some of the problems that they may have encountered during the past year or maybe just the past months. They like to clear away the cobwebs before they start their vacation, so they aren't spending valuable leisure time and money hashing over seemingly insurmountable problems.

Use your good sense. You *know* when the eggshell walking is becoming more and more a way of life. You *know* when you are back to square one in being able to deal with your true feelings. You *know* when you begin to clam up because expressions of how you really feel might start another unpleasant tiff.

Finally, when you believe that you are consistently distancing from the one you love, you can count on the fact that a tune-up is in the wings, waiting to be called on stage. By this, I mean you need a tune-up when you find yourself getting emotionally more detached from your alcoholic, not really caring to work on problems that are cropping up in the relationship and feeling more and more as if there is little hope that change for the better will ever happen.

This distancing is a harmful process; it tells the alcoholic that his reward for trying lifelong sobriety is to lose touch with you. It tells *you* that it is too painful to deal with the reality of the situation, and so you begin carefully and maybe even subconsciously to pull away from the relationship, to make it easier to leave it completely in case things "don't work out."

When you feel either of you begin this distancing, don't delay! Get your emotional cars on the rack for that tune-up. Distancing needs to be confronted and dealt with as soon as it becomes a habit, as soon as you realize that you are using this method as a *tool* in itself, preventing you from taking the risks necessary to make your relationship work.

The idea of getting well together is to *stay* well together. Don't let foolish pride prevent you from reaching out as many times as necessary for professional help in the form of a short-term tune-up. It's just the thing to help keep a relationship engine humming!

Part III

FACING FAILURE—
THE PRESENT
CONTINUED

13

The Intervention

"What can I do if my alcoholic doesn't *want* help?"

That is one of the most frequently asked questions. You've been there before. You've had that helpless feeling that you are caught in some kind of living hell, seeing your alcoholic get worse and worse and feeling more and more helpless to do anything about it. Enter crisis intervention.

Simply stated, this is a method that can be used to lure the alcoholic into a confrontational setting, present him or her with a list of alcoholic behaviors that have affected the person presenting, and offer a set of consequences to the alcoholic that all point to his or her entering some kind of treatment.

The term *crisis* is applicable, because intervention should be used only as a *last* resort. I don't believe in letting up on the other avenues of communication that can be worked between you and your lovable alcoholic to urge him or her to seek help.

But when all leads have been exhausted, when you are really up against the stubborn person who continues to maintain, "*I've* got no problem! It's *you* that has the problem!" I think you must consider the intervention as a tool for you to get help, even when help isn't being sought by the alcoholic. I am going to rely heavily on what I described as the heart and soul of an intervention in my earlier book, *Sitting in the Bay Window*.

While *Bay Window* is geared specifically to parents of young alcoholics who are facing the problems of alcohol-

121

ism, the *methods* of the intervention remain the same. So, let's review them together for *you*, the significant other.

First of all, the intervention is *not* an act of cruelty. You are getting your loved one help when it isn't wanted, as an act of *love*. If you really didn't care about this person, you could just let him drink himself to death. But understand that you are going to be the victim of the wrath of the alcoholic.

The most often heard remark will be along the lines of "You set me up." Of course, that's *exactly* what you have done, because the alcoholic didn't take any action to help herself! No matter; that particular anger will go two ways. One, it will dissipate and turn into gratitude to you for the action you took. Two, it will remain as the *principal* reason the alcoholic continues to drink! Hopefully, the first is the particular road that you will travel—together!

An intervention requires the use of a professional, and I strongly urge you to seek such a person as opposed to trying to do this yourself. You *must*, in my opinion, use a trained and skilled interventionist. The reason? The amateur or well-meaning doctor, pastor, or perhaps other family friend—in other words, someone not *specifically* trained for this work—can do a great deal of emotional damage, not only to the "victim" of the intervention, but to the people who have been taking part.

As I have said many times before to people who balk at the use of a professional for interventions, "You are playing with human emotions that don't just involve the alcoholic. *Everyone* who participates is affected, whether the intervention is a success or a failure."

As long as I've brought up that word *failure*, perhaps this is a good time to face that specter for what it really is. When I say *failure* I mean the inability of the intervention process to guide the alcoholic into treatment, into A.A., or into anything else that might help save the abuser's life from the ravages of alcohol.

The person being intervened might very well listen to what everyone has to say; hear all the consequences that are proposed, including the most severe one that *you* offer; and then quite deliberately get up and leave the room with a wave of his hand and a "To hell with all of you!" farewell.

I've seen it happen. Fortunately, of the many interventions I have conducted, the bulk have been successful. That's not because of any necessarily brilliant skills on my part as an interventionist. Mostly, it's because the *power* of the whole procedure is so overwhelmingly in favor of the person agreeing to enter treatment.

If the subject does get up and leave the room, however, and you believe that the intervention has failed, *no one* must try to stop him! Nor should anyone make any other move except to let the person go. You must realize that you are dealing with an angry, hurt, and confused person at this stage. This person feels as if the whole world is against him because of his drinking.

For the moment, after the subject has walked out on you, it is *you* and the other family members who may have participated in the intervention that need help. I try to schedule appointments for individual, conjoint, and family therapy sessions as soon as possible after an unsuccessful intervention.

A family session of at least one hour should take place *right then and there,* as soon as the intervention is completed, just to give the family the opportunity to deal with their feelings both about the failure of the intervention and about what plans need to be made *now* to get help.

If the alcoholic *has* left the room, usually people think of getting some help through the courts. Well, you are not going to get a whole lot of help, in spite of what you may think. There is a common misconception that spouses, or anyone else for that matter, can just "put somebody away." It doesn't quite work that way!

This is sort of a good news/bad news situation. In most states, a court order to *hold and treat* an alcoholic can be secured with the assistance of a physician or perhaps an officer of the court. That's the good news. But the bad news is that this "hold and treat" is good for just twenty-four hours, or perhaps two to four days of detoxification.

Even if a patient enters a hospital or an outpatient

facility for treatment, there is nothing the court can do to make him or her *stay*, unless there is a clear and present danger that the person is harmful to himself (suicidal) or to others (homicidal).

The staff at any facility will do everything possible to talk your alcoholic out of leaving, but if the abuser *really* wants to go, he will go! The discharge paper may indicate that the patient left AMA (against medical advice), but he will be gone nevertheless!

One of the major problems of a failed intervention is that you may have lost the opportunity to approach the alcoholic with the idea of getting help for some time. You will have used up all your trump cards, and there won't be many selling points left to get the alcoholic into treatment of one kind or another.

I want to restress that treatment should include getting the alcoholic into the fellowship of A.A., not just formalized treatment programs. However, in most cases that require the use of an intervention, the alcoholic is probably sick enough to require hospitalization, followed by long-term outpatient treatment.

Now, let's get into the intervention itself: the components of one and what's involved for both you and the other people who are to be involved in the process.

These are the general steps I use for intervention:

1. Exploration
2. Education
3. Consequences
4. Rehearsal
5. Final Dress Rehearsal
6. Intervention
7. Family Follow-Up

An intervention calls into play professionals, family members, friends, coworkers, and employers, working in a concentrated setting of love, care, and concern, to forcefully guide the alcoholic into seeking treatment.

In my opinion, an intervention works only when the consequences set up by those involved are so firm that the alcoholic is fearful of what he or she will lose if treatment is not sought. You'll get the drift as you read through this chapter. For now, let's review the process step by step.

The Exploration

Quite simply, this step is taken when someone who cares has had to make contact with a professional or has been referred to such a person or place in the hope of getting help for someone who doesn't want it. What is required now is for those interested parties to get together and explore the ways and means of the intervention.

Remember, the "victim" is not aware of what you are thinking of doing! The element of surprise is one of the most successful "weapons" of an intervention; any hints that something is afoot will defuse the intervention, removing most or all of its impact.

It's time to state emphatically that an intervention is *not* an act of cruelty! It is an honest, forthright, and meaningful expression of love for the sick individual. You are not making this critical maneuver because you hate, but because you love! Armed with that understanding, the professional you have consulted will want to gather the immediate family members together for an exploratory talk. Some of the questions that will be posed in this first meeting should be:

1. Who will be involved?
2. Where will the intervention be held?
3. Where will the person enter treatment (in-hospital, residential, or outpatient)?
4. How will the subject be brought or "lured" to the intervention?
5. Is intervention the only option that is left?

I stress the last point because I feel strongly that when a family tries an intervention and it fails, long-term discouragement and setbacks set in and become very hard to overcome. That's why, in the exploration stage, all parties involved should be urged to give their views; all of the doubts and the fears should be expressed at this first meeting.

Fears? You bet! An intervention is a scary thing for most families, because *it may not be successful!* The people who will be involved will feel like they are all back at square one in dealing with the alcoholic. Let's put that fear aside and discuss it after looking at the other steps.

The selection of the kind of treatment program to be the target for the intervention will depend on the assessment made by the professionals you are working with. They will listen to stories of the behavior of the alcoholic or alcohol abuser, the kinds of difficulties that have resulted from the alcoholic behavior, and the possible physical characteristics and problems that might be a part of the picture.

Whether treatment will be sought as an inpatient or outpatient, for example, will be determined largely by evaluating which is likely to be more successful. Will your alcoholic be better off being removed from his or her environment and admitted to a hospital for a period of time, or will he or she be able to function in an outpatient setting, maintaining job, school, or other activities while obtaining treatment?

The selection of a residential program will also be the focus of the professional staff with whom you are working. Just believe this: The object of an intervention is to get help for someone who doesn't want it, and the professionals will want that person to enter the program or facility that they believe has the best chance of working for him or her!

Those of us who provide intervention services certainly do not make the selection of our own facility a necessary ingredient for performing the intervention. Quite the contrary! Many times I have been involved in performing the intervention for a family in which the objective was to get their loved one into a hospital or residential facility the family chose.

Cost of treatment programs vary, and the professional will help you find the ones that fit your means, including the sliding-scale (ability-to-pay) and public programs.

The site of the intervention is extremely important. The general rule should not be to avoid all "safe grounds," where the alcoholic could bolt from the session and seek safety in his or her own room. Usually, a friend's or neighbor's house, a sibling's residence, or perhaps a church setting will be chosen as the place for the intervention.

Once the place has been determined, how is the lure to work? No one is going to be invited just to come and hear how he needs to be whisked off to treatment, so some sort of subterfuge is, unfortunately, necessary. This is where many family members bog down in the intervention process. They feel as if they are part of a "Judas act," a betrayal of the one they love.

When you talk about "luring" the person to the intervention, what you are really discussing is *how* to get the person to the place. Usually, a family member will suggest something that will give the professional a clue to explore further with you. It may be a birthday party or celebration of some other kind, which the alcoholic would be expected to attend anyhow. It obviously would *not* be the *alcoholic's* birthday, but rather that of another family member or friend.

Pretexts of needing repair work done, helping with a specific chore, or seeing a new movie on television are some of the other methods that can be used to help lure the person to his or her own intervention.

Now the question of who will be involved draws our attention. You have a place, a facility for treatment, and a method of getting the person to the intervention. The people who are to be actually involved are, of course, principal to the success of an intervention.

Should all the brothers and sisters, the grandparents, uncles and aunts, cousins, etc., be involved? Probably not! It's too unwieldy and too dangerous because of the heavy emotional trip that an intervention involves.

Uppermost in the selection process should be the family and friends who are (1) the people of greatest influence on the alcoholic's life and (2) the people who have the strongest consequences to impose.

Grandma and Grandpa may be very important, but

they may not carry as much clout as, say, a younger brother or sister who is being more directly affected by the alcoholic's behavior. Get the idea? That's why this exploration session is held, to be able to sort the methods, the people, and the ways that will help ensure the best chance for success of the intervention. I find six to nine persons, plus the interventionist best. Other professionals will have their own criteria and will make them known to you.

An employer who will have direct effect on the livelihood of the alcoholic and who is *aware of and supportive* of treatment for the alcoholic is a valuable member of the intervention team. Close and supportive friends need to be considered and accepted or rejected, all with the same eye to their *sphere of influence* and the *strength of their consequence*. Thus, a sweetheart who will threaten to end the relationship if treatment is not sought by the alcoholic is an obviously stronger choice than a younger sibling who says, "You can't borrow my things anymore." (This may be the sibling's strongest consequence, but it's basically ineffective.)

The exploration session may contain many elements other than the ones discussed so far. Each case is specific and will breed its own set of problems. Your professional interventionist will help you talk out your fears and concerns.

You may have wondered about my continued use of the terms *professional* and *interventionist*. You *must* use a trained person to do this job! The amateur—the colleague or well-meaning doctor, the pastor or other family friend—who is not specifically and specially trained for intervention can cause a great deal of damage!

You are playing with human emotions that involve not just the alcoholic but everyone who is participating in the intervention, and trusting that process to the untrained is simply a very bad, very dangerous, and explosive decision.

The Education

In this step you should be shown a film or videotape of a dramatized intervention and perhaps given some very basic education about what the disease is doing to the family as well as to the alcoholic. The education session will also probably focus on weeding out some of the original people who were slated to take part. Many times, after viewing or hearing about an intervention, some individuals decide not to participate, or it becomes very clear to everyone else that those people should not participate.

For example, daughters or sons (in older-adult interventions) who simply can't bring themselves to "turn against" Mom or Dad, often eliminate themselves from the intervention. The more powerful the educational presentation, the more likely it is that you may lose some of these people. This is the point at which it *should* happen; don't wait for the actual intervention to find out that someone can't go on with his or her role.

Whatever the education that is planned for the people who have been selected initially, it will be this session that will lead to the next step.

The Consequences

This is, at first sight, a difficult step. The consequences here are the kinds of appropriate action that people can take or threaten to take if the alcohol abuser refuses help. Remember, the example of the younger sibling's refusal to lend her belongings is not a very good consequence.

At this stage the interventionist asks each member of the team to make a list of alcohol-related incidents involving the subject of the intervention and the team member. This list cannot be made at this session; it's something everyone needs to think about alone and be prepared to bring to the first rehearsal.

Along with that list (sometimes called the *indictments*) are specific things that each individual is willing to say he or she will do, *if* the subject refuses to seek help.

In the cases of individuals seeking to get alcoholic spouses into treatment, the most powerful weapon of consequence is the threat of divorce. The key, of course, is that the spouse *must be determined to carry out the threat!*

It's totally ineffective for you to bring in a list of consequences that you have no intention of carrying out! As parents, your most powerful consequence is probably to tighten the financial screws to the maximum. A typical example might be a father telling his son in intervention that, unless the son gets help, *all* financial help he has been providing will stop.

Suppose a traffic citation (DUI—Driving Under the Influence) has been issued as a result of an alcoholic incident; the resultant loss of the use of other family vehicles then becomes a good consequence. Other brothers or sisters can refuse to drive or lend their cars to the offender unless the offender seeks help. Get the idea?

An employer has the best shot at putting his consequences where his mouth is. "If you don't get help, Larry, I'm going to suspend [or fire] you. You're one of my best employees, but I can't see you continuing with us in the condition you're in!"

Even the youngest members of the family who are going to participate in the intervention can offer consequences, and, in fact, these are sometimes the most touching. I recall one little guy, just seven years old, who tearfully told his older alcohol-abusing brother that if he didn't "go to get help," he wouldn't "ever let you work on my stamp collection again!" It didn't seem like much, but the way the child brought it off in his own halting, whispery voice was a real gut-wrencher and helped turn the trick!

Once again, the most important element of the consequences is that nothing can be used or stated as a consequence that the person is not absolutely prepared to carry out! All of the teeth are pulled from a consequence when it is never brought into play. In the case of a mate threatening divorce, I will not proceed with an intervention until the mate has actually seen or contacted a lawyer or at least can show a standard petition form for dissolution of marriage. If he or she can produce some kind of evidence of serious intent, then the consequence is allowed.

Such actions can always be put on hold; most attorneys who are aware of the circumstances will know and understand the reasoning for using such a powerful weapon. I have used a family attorney as a member of the intervention to present a consequence to a young adult male being forcefully guided into treatment.

The attorney was there to represent with forceful action the consequence delivered by a grandmother who was unable to attend the intervention due to illness. The attorney read a letter from the grandmother instructing him to "substantially alter her bequest" to the young man, should he refuse to "straighten out his life and give up drink." The young man loved his grandmother very much; she had raised him for most of his life, and it was a powerful consequence. It wasn't just the potential loss of money from her, but the scathing attack of the letter delivered (through an attorney) that helped turn the tide toward treatment.

Members of the intervention team should *not* share what their consequences are until the next step of the process, the rehearsal.

The Rehearsal

At this meeting all are assembled in a room the interventionist has made available, usually not the actual room where the intervention will take place. The members of the group are seated in a semi-circle facing two chairs. One of those chairs is for the interventionist, and the other is for the subject of the intervention.

Since this is a rehearsal, obviously the subject is not present; the empty chair just represents the subject. One at a time, the individual members of the intervention team read from their prepared lists. Each list should be headed with the phrase, "Larry [or whomever], I *love you* and I *care about you!*" This phrase is used by everyone in his or her turn. It should be underlined and is *absolutely* the first thing that is said by each person.

The person speaking then continues by giving specific *alcohol-related incidents of behavior* in which the person and the subject were involved. Give specific times, dates, and places. For example, Mother says, "Larry, last week when my bridge group was here you came into the room. The smell of beer on your breath was overpowering, and I was *humiliated!* You were obviously drunk, and it was only three in the afternoon!" Or, from a younger brother: "Larry, when my friend Jeff came to spend the night Saturday, you came into our room and started messing up our Monopoly game! You were drunk, and I was ashamed of you!"

You get the idea. But each speaker begins with the "love you/care about you" phrase. One by one, each speaker gives his list of "grievances," being careful that they are all alcohol-related and documented by specific time, date, and place. At the conclusion of the list of each person's grievances, the consequence is given.

The interventionist will suggest that each person of the group closely watch the member who is speaking. This focuses the attention on what's being said. It will be *hard* on you. You will hear things from your own group that you never knew, perhaps, and it will bring tears of hurt and anguish! This is the reason for the rehearsal. It lets you get the surprises out in the open; it lets you deal with the enormity of what you are about to do, namely, share feelings openly!

No matter what happens, *no matter how hard it is*, no member of the group should get up or go to the person speaking when that person falters, cries, or otherwise falls apart while giving his or her grievances/consequence list. The interventionist will stress this, but you need to be prepared. You will want to go to the person who is crying or sobbing, but you must not! A large part of the effectiveness of the intervention lies in the fact that *all* group members become aware of what the subject's alcoholic behavior has done to each member of this group who loves the alcoholic!

You will be guided by whatever educational session materials you have used and by your interventionist in other fine details to be worked out in the rehearsal.

The Final Dress Rehearsal

For the final dress rehearsal you will probably be in the actual place in which the intervention is to be staged. Your lists have been pared down, with some items added or eliminated, and some people may have been eliminated since the first rehearsal because of either their inability to deliver their consequences or the lack of strength behind their consequences.

In the final dress rehearsal all details of how the subject will be controlled are carefully explained by the interventionist. He or she will have some prepared, memorized script to use for this purpose. Here's what I use:

"Larry, your family and your friends are here today because they love you and they care about you. I want you to sit here with me and listen to what they have to say. I don't want you to interrupt, but I'll give you a chance to speak later!"

That's just an idea of the general tone an interventionist might use to get things rolling. Each person has his or her own way of doing things, but you get the drift of how it will sound. The sixth step of the process is the actual intervention.

The Intervention

Now the rehearsal, the questioning, the doubts, the fears and anxieties come into focus. This "D-Day" is critical, emotional, and utterly draining! This is it! The intervention itself will probably take an hour. The subject has been "duped," by whatever means, into walking or being led into a roomful of people.

The group has already been assembled, in their chairs, in their proper order of speaking. This order of speaking has been worked out in your rehearsals and is designed to be the most effective sequence. Let me assure you that this setting has a powerful *shock value* for the subject the moment he or she enters that room!

I never fail to be amazed at the element of surprise that works for us! The alcoholic doesn't immediately understand or comprehend what is happening. The subject thought he was coming to a particular function or party or whatever has been used as the "bait" and suddenly finds himself in a room with family, friends, employer, sweetheart, pastor, and a stranger who is telling him, basically, to "sit down and be quiet and listen to what these people have to say!"

It's mind-boggling! It's one of the reasons that intervention has to be carefully planned, thought about, rehearsed, and staged for maximum effectiveness! The pure emotion of the event is swept through the room like a powerful gale, and only hearing the statement "We love you and we care about you!" over and over reassures the entire group that what they are doing is not cruel but loving, caring, and concerned. This intervention will be difficult, so don't treat it lightly. It is, nonetheless, a very effective tool *when all other means have been tried and have failed*.

Just as in the rehearsal, it is of paramount importance that you avoid leaving your chair and running into the arms of the subject! The subject may burst into tears while he or she listens to the alcoholic incidents that have touched the family member or friend reciting them; he or she may cry out of sheer empathy at seeing a brother, a sister, parent, or sweetheart sitting there sobbing while pouring out their grievances and consequences.

However, at no time must the subject be allowed contact with any group member until he or she has agreed to enter treatment. The interventionist will gently restrain the subject from leaving his chair; *you* will have to restrain yourselves!

When all the group has been heard from, the interventionist will tell the subject what his or her choices are: enter the treatment selected or face the consequences that this roomful of people have given.

The Family Follow-Up

Finally, we get to the last section of this process, the family follow-up. It's important that, *regardless* of the outcome of the intervention, the family members who have participated in the intervention get a chance to deal with their feelings. Some very heavy emotions have been expressed in the hour of the intervention. Even if the subject has refused treatment, the family members need the opportunity to deal with their feelings.

So, the intervention becomes another tool for you to use, albeit sparingly and with great caution. As a significant-other person in the life of an alcoholic, you become a focal point, a sort of fulcrum that sways the balance between sickness and health. when you are willing to examine and use the consequences that may be developed for an intervention.

We have talked for so much of this book about your not having power to make your alcoholic well, and that still holds true. But the power of the consequences, the *indictments* of an intervention, can be mighty indeed!

You are now, presumably, poised on the brink of a decision about whether an intervention is the *only* way left for you to confront the one you love. Take the advice of the folk hero frontiersman and congressman, Davy Crockett: "Be always sure you're right—then go ahead."

14

When They Return to Drink

You might not have wanted to think about the possibility of your recovering alcoholic returning to drink someday. Nevertheless, it is a fact of life. Alcoholics are always just one drink away from the next drunk for as long as they live. That's the nature of this disease for which there is no cure.

So that's the bottom line. Now you know, and therefore you needn't be overly afraid of it! Many times a relapse can be therapeutic. Why? Because it helps break down the *denial* that your alcoholic has been using as a shield to say, "I'll bet I can learn to *control* my drinking . . . I'll quit after one or two!" The alcoholic *never* quits after one or two, but instead drinks until getting drunk. If a relapse happens, the person denying his or her alcoholism gets a clear message that there is no such thing as "controlled drinking" for the alcoholic.

Relapses don't "just happen." We know that the alcoholic plans, albeit sometimes subconsciously, to begin to drink again. I am always amused when a patient shares with me or with a group "just finding herself with a glass in her hand!"

The relapse syndrome, as it is called by some, doesn't just materialize out of thin air. It is carefully orchestrated by the alcoholic, and when the relapse *does* occur, there is always a lame-duck excuse of being caught in some situation or other that made turning to drink the only possible solution for the problem.

At our treatment center we refer to this process of

building up to drink as "having a BUD" (*BUD* meaning "building up to drink"), a phrase I think was first used in one of our lectures by my close friend and colleague, Liz Telford, MSW.

The dynamics are as clear as signposts that you, the significant other, can read. The problem is that you stare at these pretty clear-cut warnings and let your *own* denial get in the way of confronting your alcoholic.

Many studies have been done to determine that there are some *patterns* to the things that alcoholics do to begin this process of having a BUD. Almost all of the data will show that every alcoholic patient left his treatment with the *intention to remain permanently sober*.

But things go wrong with the best of intentions in this world, and when a relapse occurs you find *yourself* almost as devastated that this thing could happen as the alcoholic is. Don't despair! The important thing is to take stock of what might have happened in these dynamics, confront the behavior, and *move on with your lives*.

Sure, you are going to have to start over with a step toward permanent sobriety. But this is not exactly like returning to square one. You both have come a long way in recovery, and what has happened might be a very helpful thing for both of you in the long run. The reason? Because a relapse points up the first step and the undeniable truth of that step in the program of A.A., which says, "We were powerless over alcohol; our lives had become unmanageable."

Alcohol the chemical, alcohol the drink, alcohol the *destroyer* is *more* powerful than your alcoholic! It is a humbling, devastating *fact* of your life, and the sooner it becomes imprinted on your mind, the more at ease you can become so you can go on with the business of living with this disease.

I do not mean to suggest that you should live with relapse after relapse; if this keeps happening, you are going to have to look once again at the original set of consequences that you may have used to get your alcoholic into treatment and A.A., way back when, before the relapse.

There are many lists of the warning signs of having a BUD. In *Sitting in the Bay Window,* I presented my own list, which I thought reflected a cross section of what was in most of the other studies that I had read, plus a few that I had developed as being unique to my own program of recovery.

For you, the significant other, I am offering a slightly different list, one that gives *you* the responsibility to see the warning signs as they present themselves. Hopefully, you will have the risk-taking capabilities by this time to do a little confronting. The purpose, of course, is for you *both* to head off a relapse before it happens. However, if one *does* occur, you must both have the courage to push ahead. You will both need to sit down and ask yourselves, "What do you think happened to cause this relapse?" (Notice I do not say, "*Why* did the drinking happen?" This phrasing sets the alcoholic to accept responsibility for the drinking—the "why" he or she drank is because they have a disease. What fell apart for them? What tools did they fail to use?) If a relapse *does* cloud your smooth path of recovery, then you need to contact the program, the therapist, the A.A. sponsor, the aftercare coordinator, etc., where you both received your treatment, support, and *sobriety*. These people are there to help you sort out the problems of the relapse and to get you started on the right track again; *use* them.

Now, let's look at the warning signs you should be aware of in your alcoholic:

1. exhaustion
2. the "pity pot"
3. pushing alcohol on others
4. trying to reform the rest of the world
5. overconfidence
6. overspending
7. the silent treatment
8. "Merlinism"
9. "pie-in-the-sky"
10. lack of interest in a structured life
11. irregular attendance at A.A., aftercare, etc.
12. impatience

* * *

There's no magic to the order of this list of warning signs of a possible relapse; you should just be aware of them all. The chances are that you will even be able to come up with some more on your own, the kinds of things that are *consistently* present when a relapse happens.

I also want to caution you about spending twenty-four hours a day in a confrontational attitude with your alcoholic. After all, people *do* have bad days, even alcoholics! Just because your husband or wife is a little grouchy (or even very grouchy!) doesn't mean that your alcoholic is having a BUD. It *does*, however, make it OK for you to watch and see if the particular behavior persists or continues to repeat. If it does, then chances are pretty good that a BUD is in the offing. Therefore, you should do a little risk taking by confronting.

Now, let's look at these warning signs one at a time, in more detail. Feel free to make whatever custom changes in them you wish to fit more closely with your situation. But remember, these signs come up *so* consistently with recovering alcoholics, and are talked about by their significant others *so* frequently, that there is strong evidence that you all can benefit from heeding them.

Exhaustion

This is a two-headed monster! It refers to both the alcoholic's symptoms of exhaustion *and* yours. When you see your alcoholic allowing himself to get overly tired or letting his general health slip, you should run up the red flag of warning. A wonderful acronym that is used worldwide in the fellowship of A.A. is *HALT*. It means don't allow yourself to get too hungry, angry, lonely, or tired.

In your case, you need to watch for the same telltale signs of your own exhaustion. You certainly need to watch for the lack of HALT in your alcoholic!

* * *

The "Pity Pot"

In my book, *The Joy of Being Sober*, I dwelled on this "magical" pot at some length, as well as including it in *Sitting in the Bay Window*. You must gather by now, with my including it here for you, that the "pity pot" is a *big* warning sign, indeed! This pity pot is a "magical" one that seems to grow wider and deeper the longer one sits on its rim! When you observe and *listen* to your alcoholic climb up on the pity pot, look out! A BUD is probably waiting in the wings!

Some phrases that can alert you that the alcoholic is climbing up to this giant pity pot are things like these:

"Why am I an alcoholic?"

"Why can't I drink like everyone else?"

"No one cares about me or what I'm trying to do!"

Watch for the pity pot for yourself, too. Don't put your own ladders up there by saying things such as, "My God! Is there no end to all this *alcohol* business?" and "I'm *so* damn tired of being the one to do all the work on this thing!" The "poor me" attitude will get you on the blind side, and you will fail to see your alcoholic heading into a possible relapse because your own view is blocked by your perch on your own pity pot!

Pushing Alcohol On Others

This is a very obvious warning sign. The alcoholic wants you to drink, to have that glass of wine with dinner that you've always enjoyed. She is practically forcing a drink into the hands of your company, the second they are in the front door. Watch this! Your alcoholic is resentful of other people "having fun" by drinking, and probably wants to drink right with you and them!

It's essential that you live a normal drinking life, if you have done so in the past. Sure, you want to be sensitive to the struggle that your alcoholic is going through, but your alcoholic will have to face the facts of life; namely, it is the alcoholic who has the problem! It is he who is in the minority, since most of the people in this country can and *do* drink with little or no problems.

The pushing of alcohol on you, when you may not particularly want it, is a BUD warning sign that spells *trouble* and needs to be confronted, if it keeps happening over and over again.

Trying to Reform the Rest of the World

Well, this ties in a lot with the warning sign above. But now your alcoholic wants *everyone* to join him in sobriety! You thought it was bad when he was pushing booze on you and all your friends; now he wants to tell all of you how bad this stuff is and asks, "When do you want to do something about *your* problem?"

It's a warning sign that also spells resentment, in that your alcoholic is realizing more and more that he can't ever drink again and simply wants a lot of company in that department.

Overconfidence

The recovering person convinces herself that there is almost nothing that can't be accomplished now that she has sobriety. Well, to an extent that's good, but it can rise up and strike when least expected. The recovering person, and consequently you, may let down his or her guard, and both of you will find this warning sign staring you right in the face!

When you observe what I call a "Superman" or "Wonder Woman" complex, be wary! This overconfidence is the kind of thing that has your alcoholic saying, "No problem with stopping at the bar every night on my way home to 'see the guys!' *They* drink, but I just have my Coke!" That may work for a while, but on a long-term basis that kind of overconfidence can lead to trouble, and you need to be on the lookout for such a warning sign.

Overspending

This is a tough one for you to pick up on. You may be noticing that your recovering person is suddenly coming home with new tools or trinkets for you and the family, which you know are expensive. There doesn't seem to be a real pattern in this; he may suggest that you have extra money because no more bottles of beer or liquor are being bought!

That sounds pretty good to you, and therefore you may miss out on the warning sign of overspending, a trait that is much too reminiscent of "setting up the house" for a round of drinks. The trap that you may fall into is the one that is *so pleased* with the sobriety that you lull *yourself* into thinking that this money can be spent for the new stereo, campers, boats, or what have you. It may be that you *can* now afford many things that your alcohol was taking away. What I want you to watch for is *compulsive* spending, which is a possible BUD in the making.

The Silent Treatment

Most significant others will pick up on this warning sign in themselves, but don't put much stock in it when it is staring at them from the recovering person. They attribute the lack of communication to many things, usually "change in personality since sobriety," "always has been sort of quiet," etc.

But when this silent treatment continues for longer periods of time, when you have been unable to get a satisfactory answer to "What's wrong, honey?" you can certainly count on the fact that your recovering person is either well into a BUD or is really working up to one.

They need to be confronted about what's going on, about what's making them bury their feelings. In short, you must say, "Let's talk about your *wanting* to drink." Don't be put off! Be persistent!

"Merlinism"

My being a fan of King Arthur and his times is what brought this warning sign into being. Merlin the magician was the one who was always supposed to have the right answers for Arthur, who could solve all of Arthur's many woes after the blush of the success of the Round Table had worn off. Well, it's the same with the recovering person. When your alcoholic is constantly bringing you this article or that about a new "sober pill" or some other such "magical cure" for alcoholism, watch out!

Alcoholism is a disease, as yet incurable. Patent medicines that appeal to the alcoholic are like trying to put Band-Aids on a major wound! It won't work, and you should be prepared to ask your alcoholic and *yourself*, "What's going on in your (our) life that makes it necessary to have alcohol to enjoy it?"

The alcoholic has to learn that there is a "joy of being sober," and I don't apologize one iota for the obvious reference to my book of that name! The alcoholic *must* learn to live life without alcohol; hence, without Merlinlike cures. Get on with the business of living and, yes, hope that medical science will someday find a method of ending this disease. In the meantime, Merlinism is to be considered a warning sign of utmost importance!

"Pie-in-the-Sky"

This warning sign ties into overconfidence, cockiness, and a lot of other things. Mostly, it refers to the alcoholic's spending a lot of time with "big schemes" instead of getting back down to earth and dealing with reality. The person who is never satisfied with his job, and who always has a "great idea" to make a fortune, is probably heading for a BUD. When you hear these grand schemes, imagine that your alcoholic has just thrown a bunch of confetti in the air. Everything that comes down in a solid ball he'll deal with! Everything else remains confetti! A BUD is imminent.

Lack of Interest in a Structured Life

This is really another way of saying that the alcoholic follows a pattern that allows him to let up on discipline, and this is very dangerous. This warning sign can come from a combination of causes, but boredom, overconfidence, and general complacency are certainly *some* of the reasons why you begin to see your alcoholic begin to get sloppy in his daily routines.

Regular hours of rising and sleeping seem to disappear. The alcoholic begins to miss appointments or forget them. You will be able to discern a definite lack of time management by your alcoholic, and tension and frustration, coupled with a lot of anxiety in doing even simple things, become apparent.

The alcoholic begins to stumble more and more on life's "mouse turds," and *you* begin to play old tapes about what more *you* can do. Watch that! Heed the warning sign and confront!

Irregular Attendance at A.A., Aftercare, Etc.

When your recovering person is missing her therapy sessions, when A.A. is no longer important, and when you are seeing less and less time devoted to personal sobriety, you can be sure that your alcoholic is setting up a BUD.

You'll begin to hear the alcoholic discount the effectiveness of treatment and A.A. There will even be periods during which you will hear the alcoholic *totally* discount the efficacy of the treatment process, protesting, "I could've done it myself!"

The recovering person using this BUD technique will start to tell you that "we can't continue to afford therapy," or "that A.A. group is a bunch that I don't have anything in common with!" (These people conveniently ignore the *most* common bond, alcoholism!)

Rationalization will be flying around your house like so many flies at a garbage can! And that's how you have to treat it. You put a lid on it with face-to-face confrontation, shooting down all the excuses and making sure *you* keep up your attendance right along with the abuser.

Impatience

Quite simply, things are not happening fast enough to suit your recovering alcoholic. The trap here is that *you* may be ignoring the same warning sign because things are not happening fast enough for you either.

When the alcohol got out of the relationship, you thought things were going to get better in a hurry, and they may not. They probably *did not* get better as quickly as you wanted. Remember that you both have spent a long time being sick; you need to spend the necessary time to get well. It won't happen overnight, and the tendency toward great impatience will have to be thwarted.

This impatience leads to a general dissatisfaction with life. Things aren't changing fast enough, so, the alcoholic states, "I might as well get drunk!" When the rationalizations and the tunnel vision about a life of sobriety set in, the alcoholic begins to believe honestly that things are "so bad now" (without the world moving at her marching step) that "if I get drunk, it couldn't be any worse!"

Your recovering person may feel pretty powerless to do anything about speeding up the process of getting well.

Well, as I said earlier, you can undoubtedly make your own list of warning signs to add to those we've been looking at. What's most important is that you *heed* these warning signs when they pop up in front of you. Like all such signs, they are designed to let you see the danger ahead.

A word about depression is in order here. I have not included that as a separate warning sign because I have found it to be so much of a constant in early stages of recovery that you are probably always aware of it. The alcoholic has to go through a grieving period; he has, after all, lost his "best friend," the bottle.

Depression is part of the price that will have to be paid for this loss and used as a means of turning the alcoholic's life around and replacing depression with happiness and joy. However, *deep* depression, and the frequency with which it may occur, should be watched carefully. When the alcoholic starts to isolate himself, when depression occurs more frequently and lasts longer, the depression becomes more disruptive in everyday life, and drinking or thoughts of drinking seem more logical than ever.

As the significant other, you can help combat these periods of depression by reinforcing the changes and wonderful times that sobriety has brought to *both* of you.

Don't discount the alcoholic's feelings of being down, but acknowledge that "it must be tough on you right now." Point out the pluses to your relationship and to his life since sobriety and pledge to work right alongside your alcoholic to help him through the period of blues.

Remember to keep HALT clearly before you as a principal guide to all the other warning signs. The general theme I have given you in this chapter is to *recognize* the warning sign and then *confront*.

If a relapse occurs, don't throw in the towel, but ask yourselves what happened and what you want to do to prevent it from happening again. You will grow in strength; you will learn new and valuable tools to help keep a BUD from happening and particularly how to put the specters of frequent relapses behind you. The trend toward having a BUD will diminish with every week and month and year of sobriety that you can notch in your belt, and that's a promise from one who should know!

15

Repeating Mistakes

Oscar Wilde once said, "Experience is the name everyone gives to their mistakes."

Well, you've certainly had a lot of experience at this stage of the game—experience in trying to live your life with an alcoholic who is either in recovery or is still actively drinking. There are times when it seems as if you cannot face another day in the kind of special hell that is reserved for the significant-other person. Yet you face up to it, carry on, and trust that things will get better.

Many times, thank God, they do! But many times, the relationship ends up on the trash heap of life, and you are off looking again for that special someone that is going to be just right for you to spend the rest of your life with, someone who will appreciate the many qualities that you bring to a relationship.

You go through the mating dance ritual of whatever particular social scene in which you operate. Then, just when things seem hopeless, when it seems that you might as well pack it in as far as finding someone, there he or she is!

All the old, good vibes crank up in you again, and you believe that there *is* a chance that you may have met someone who will rescue you from a life of being alone again. Then it happens. Ever so gently, easily, and almost without fanfare of any kind, you begin to recognize that this person has many of the same qualities as the alcoholic you have been separated from.

Perhaps you have managed an introduction or a party

date, or you are finding good chemistry dancing or having dinner with this new person. You may begin to notice that she is drinking a little too fast; at least it appears that way to you. It seems that she is able to put down two drinks to your one, and as time goes on you have begun to pick up on the mood swings that seem to occur with this new person, the more alcohol that is consumed. But things seem so rosy!

You turn the other cheek, literally, in the glow and indeed the afterglow of the newfound relationship. If the specter of overdrinking appears on the scene, you probably have chalked it up to the natural rush of a new relationship and all that goes with such things.

"I don't think he *really* drinks all *that* much!" you find yourself saying to the image in the mirror the morning after another date with the new person. You find yourself making comparisons very quickly. This new person certainly *handles* his drinks better than the last person who had the "drinking problem."

This new relationship seems to you to have a lot more going for it than the last. *This* person treats you better, even if she seems to drink a little too much "every now and then." And so it goes.

You find yourself burrowing deeper into the old tape of denial, even though all the red lights, flashing arrows, and warning buzzers have been going off in your head for a long time—ever since you first had that old feeling in the pit of your stomach!

You have found yourself another alcoholic! Oh my God!

"Why, oh *why* do I keep doing this?" you wail!

"What is *wrong* with me that I attract *this* kind?"

"Why does this keep happening to me?"

"Won't I *ever* learn?"

So goes the litany of your life! Please notice that I've overlooked, just this once, that here you are using that forbidden word *why* again. That's OK! I wanted to make a point about the hopelessness that you feel when you realize that you have not too gingerly stepped on the edge of that old alcoholic silken web again, and you have just glimpsed the spider on his way down to get you!

But the point of this whole chapter is to make you confront the fact that this *really* happens to more significant others than you can imagine. I've told you before, but it's worth repeating here: The brutal statistics tell us two out of three women who lose an alcoholic by death or divorce or separation *end up with another alcoholic*.

The male significant-other person is more inclined to be a little more cautious in selecting another alcoholic, but he will definitely be *attracted* to another one! There are a lot of dynamics at work here, so don't think that you simply are a "different breed of cat." It is helpful to understand, however, what *does* seem to make another alcoholic attractive to you.

First of all, you have been able to make denial such a part of your life that you totally ignore all those little warning signs. You allow the "hooking in" to this new person to get established. By the time the denial tape is replaced with one of reality, it's often too late.

This happens because of one new aspect of your personality as a significant other that we have saved for discussion until now: you are a very *needy* person. It is this incredible need that makes you so vulnerable to picking up another sick alcoholic to nurture.

And that's point number two: you are able to nurture and tend a sick person better than most folks, because that's one of the main ways that you meet your own needs. I call this the "wounded animal syndrome," and I've seen it so many times in patients that it's almost a predictable part of the behavior pattern that presents itself at the early stages of treatment.

This syndrome simply means that you have the habit of seeing a wounded animal, say a bird, lying at your feet; you pick it up and devote hours and hours to tending its broken wing or drying its rain-soaked feathers. You feed it, warm it, *nurture* it, in a word, hoping that it will get well enough to fly around in the living rooms of your life, chirping away its merry songs of praise and thanks!

But when it doesn't, when the wounded bird doesn't

get as well, doesn't fly as far, or sing as prettily, you keep thinking that there is *something else* that you could have done to make it better. So you go out and look for another wounded animal, vowing that now you know exactly what you did wrong before, and *this* time you will do it right.

Well, you can just feel the tapes of all your past seven deadly sins slip back into playing position with that one, can't you? Here you are again, believing that you have the *power* to heal another wounded animal.

Now you know! There *is* something special about you! You meet your own needs by nursing a sick alcoholic. When another alcoholic appears in your life, you immediately jump into the fray and start trying to figure out what this new wounded bird will need from you to get better.

Here's the problem with the wounded animal syndrome. The wounded bird never really does get well enough to leave, to fly off on his own, as long as he continues drinking actively, and that keeps you in the alcoholic's power! So what do you do about all this? Does reading about this behavior of yours make you angry? It should! You know that it's true. You know that, over and over, in spite of all the vows of "never again" that you cry aloud, you end up back in a relationship with another alcoholic, even though this time you are convinced it will be different. It won't!

The truth is you will only exchange one set of old alcoholic problems for a set of new alcoholic problems. Your wounded bird might do some things a little better or a little differently, but he or she will still not be able to fly, sing, or provide you with the happiness you are seeking.

There's an important key to what makes you do this. You are *looking to another person to provide your happiness, instead of being a whole person on your own*.

"Well, sure I am!" you say indignantly. "Isn't that what *everyone* does in life?"

To an extent, of course, they do. We all look to someone or several other people in our lives to *help* provide the elements that we call *happiness*. But the truly healthy person does not look to a single other person to provide *all* of the nurturing, all of the needs, and all of the wants that will lead to feeling happy.

What makes the alcoholic so attractive to you is that he presents so much good raw material to work with! When you get hooked up with another wounded bird you can hardly wait to change him. You see so much wonderful *potential* for your own happiness—and, incidentally, for your happiness as a couple—that you can't wait to get to the healing process!

So, once again, just as you were doing with the first alcoholic, you overlook all the telltale signs, all the warning signals that we have talked about, and you rationalize the hell out of the new relationship. You do this because it is *you* that is so needy.

It should become obvious to you by now that I'm leading up to wanting you to do some more of that awful risk taking, that scary process we have been looking at through the course of this book.

To take risks will mean that you have to concentrate on making yourself a whole person, not counting on this new alcoholic to answer so many of your needs. Whether it's a new alcoholic or not is really not the issue. You need to learn to be a whole person no matter what or who comes into your life, or you will continue to look to another wounded bird over and over again to supply the nurturing you so desperately need in your life.

It's risky and it's scary. You simply need to examine the fact that you have missed some nurturing, probably in childhood, that makes you look to another sick person to supply that missing ingredient. If you are the adult child of an alcoholic, you already know that you missed the full attention of the alcoholic parent; you grew up in an alcoholic home where nurturing was devoted primarily to meeting the needs of the alcoholic, not the rest of the family members who were caught in his or her web.

Don't confuse the lack of nurturing with the lack of love. You could very well have been raised in a home where there was love and still missed the nurturing. And nurturing is the element that helps to raise you, train you, educate you, and provide the necessary ingredients for your survival as a complicated human organism.

If your father was alcoholic, you missed a certain portion of your childhood, when having a father was the most important thing in your life! The alcoholics toward which you tend to gravitate seem to represent the missing father of your life. They, in their wounded bird state, present an opportunity for you to lavish love, care, and attention. The payoff for you, of course, is that you *hope* they will return this love, care, and attention, thus making up for the nurturing you missed from the alcoholic father. When they fail to do that, you start the search all over again!

It works the same way, with some variations, if your mother was alcoholic. A man may continue to seek and find alcoholic women, over and over again, because they are so helpless and sick that the man feels wanted, needed, and important in being able to care for his wounded bird. He may have been too young, weak, or incapable of doing this for his alcoholic mother.

I think you can overcome this wounded bird syndrome. It will take a considerable amount of courage, but it can be done, and you will be a better individual for it! It simply amounts to your willingness to *recognize* the symptoms and traits of the alcoholic that you continue to put up blinders against, *confront* those traits early in the relationship, and *avoid* the entanglement altogether, *until he or she has made a concentrated effort toward recovery through treatment and aftercare*.

In the meantime, it is *you* who must set about becoming less needy. You must learn that it's better to be physically alone than to go through the loneliness that an alcoholic partner forces on you. You must begin to develop the latent skills and talents, the ambitions and the drives that you always wanted, to help transform yourself from a needy person seeking another wounded bird to a healthy and then *happy* person.

When you are the maker of your own happiness, it is *you* that reaps the most rewards from the labor that went into the project. Specifically, I want you to ask yourself if this might not be the time you have waited for to reenter or start a college course or two. Is *this* the time that you can go back and complete something that you already started, something that you dropped in order to tend your last wounded bird?

I see a number of our patients who have the burning desire to complete college degrees that they began years ago. Others simply would like to pick up a class or two in something, not even aiming for a degree program.

"What's stopping you?" I ask, and then I listen to a whole bunch of lame excuses. Well, when you combine this lame-duck attitude with the wounded bird syndrome that is naturally yours, you can see that nothing moves forward! It only stays locked firmly in neutral, which keeps you as sick as the bird you are trying vainly to make well.

So you risk a few things. You make up your mind that you're going to give *yourself* some nurturing. You *can* pick up that class in computers you have been toying with, or learn sewing, or ballroom dancing (no, you don't have to have a partner; one will be supplied!), or perhaps take flying lessons.

I don't care what you do to start this self-nurturing. What I care about is that you recognize the need for it and do something about it. Don't let the excuse of "I can't afford it!" get in the way and block the playing of this new tape. You undoubtedly have all sorts of free educational and vocational opportunities in the community in which you live. If they are not free, they are at least affordable, and in many cases channels for financial aid are available to you.

Advanced schooling is, of course, just one of many options. The exercise program that you have always planned to undertake is still waiting there for you. Reentry into the world of the living through some organized sports activities, such as softball, basketball, or bowling, is yours for the asking!

What has become of your spiritual life lately? Have you avoided church or temple so long that you feel like a stranger in the place of worship where you may have spent many happy and peaceful hours before? Get back to it! It is a ready source for the nurturing that you so badly need, and it is, of course, absolutely free!

There is an entire gamut of activities that can be run. Have you wanted to be a teacher's aid? Has the possibility of becoming a day care mom crossed your mind? Do you want to learn woodworking or be able to fix your car by yourself? When was the last time you yearned to have "just a tiny part" in the community theater productions of your town?

Is there a 4-H group in need of a leader in your town? Have you the desire to get into scouting as an adult? When was the last time you thought of taking up ceramics, painting, or creative writing? Have you thought about keeping a diary as a basis for some possible short stories or perhaps the beginnings of the poetry you always liked to write but wouldn't let anyone see?

All of these things, and hundreds more, are there waiting for you, for the expense of a little effort on your part. Actually, it requires a *lot* of effort for you to want to break out of the wounded bird syndrome, but break out you must, if you are ever going to look to yourself as the primary source of your happiness.

You have been a *taker* of happiness, when you need to become a *producer*! George Bernard Shaw, in *Candida*, reminds us, "We have no more right to consume happiness without producing it than to consume wealth without producing it."

It is obvious that the number one producer of your own happiness must be you. When you rely on another person to do it, you are only opening yourself to more disappointment, hurt, anger, despair, and all those other things that contribute to your being miserable instead of being happy.

It is imperative that you set out to make a whole person of yourself so that you are well enough and strong enough to be able to give some of your energy to those who may need it without robbing you of your permanent supply. Picking up another wounded bird diverts you from the process of becoming a whole person yourself. It tells you falsely that you can make someone else well and, in the process, find the nurturing that you sadly need to make yourself well and happy.

The whole and well you will not see the wounded bird as another challenge. Instead, you will devote your energies to surrounding yourself with those people who do not need to drain you of your permanent supplies of life's gifts in order to compensate for the lack in their lives. You do not need to "rescue" another alcoholic who is not interested in rescuing himself!

You will need to avoid the siren song of the wounded bird and listen instead for the clear and beautiful sounds that come from your own achievements. No one likes to think of living a life alone, but you need to be willing to face that possibility, rather than find yourself back in a situation where you and only you are doing the work to make someone else well.

It is a bold journey, perhaps frightening, yet necessary. I urge you to undertake it, if for some reason you have lost your alcoholic relationship of the present. For you to get involved with another alcoholic will be very easy, and that's the thing you need to understand. You have a need, you see, and you have followed a pattern of looking to the wounded bird to answer that need. It will be so easy for you to do it again and again, unless you are willing to break the bondage that being needy has wrapped you in.

Don't be afraid! You will find that even the smallest accomplishments that you make as a liberated significant other will flourish and grow into bigger rewards for your life. There is nothing quite like the strength that is to be found in being a whole person, but it is a search you must willingly conduct for yourself.

Take the guidelines of all we have been discussing and be honest with yourself. Do you really *want* to be in the spider's enticing web again? Of course not! Making the effort to provide your own happiness and to break out of the mold of being needy, of looking for nurturing in the wounded bird syndrome, will be rewarded over and over again!

Promise yourself never to become involved again without heeding the warning signs, confronting the behaviors, and determining the risks of continued involvement. This is a plea to urge you to receive the therapy and treatment for yourself, from professionals, Al-Anon, aftercare, group work, and individual work in the dark and difficult areas of your life that have kept you trapped in the midst of sickness of an alcoholic relationship for such a long time!

Without treatment, and the knowledge of the disease and its effects upon you, you will continue to be a victim of this wounded bird syndrome. Once you have tasted the fruits of your victory, of ridding yourself of the neediness of your life, you will never again want to taste the bitter fruit that is carried in the beak of the wounded bird.

16

Facing Possible
Separation or Divorce

"There's *never* been a divorce in my family!"

"I don't think I can handle the idea of a divorce!"

"I'll just *tell* him that I'm going to file. Won't that do it?"

"My family! My God, my family'll just *kill* me if I get a divorce!"

A familiar bell probably went off in your brain as you read these typical statements that have been gasped out in my office by significant others, contemplating the dreaded action of separation or divorce.

I say *gasped* because they generally are breathtaking thoughts. When those thoughts are actually put into words, they almost cause the speaker to hyperventilate. The fact that the significant other may have been thinking about separation and/or divorce for some time doesn't matter. When you are actually confronted with the idea of turning those thoughts into action, it becomes frightening.

Actually, it isn't as scary as it sounds, nor do the actions of separation and divorce necessarily mean that you are permanently ending the relationship you have had with your alcoholic. What it does mean is this: you are determined that some drastic jolt to the relationship may be necessary to dramatize your feelings. These are feelings of hopelessness with the situation and feelings of anger that you should ever have to reach this stage. The mere fact that separation or divorce seems to be the only answer doesn't alter the fact that you are angry because it appears to be the one option remaining.

157

Over and over you have been racking your brain, seeking some solution to the problem that will allow you to pick up the phone and make that first terrifying call to an attorney. But alas, you keep ending up at the same spot in your thinking; you've *tried* everything else, and it seems that this is the only way left.

You've probably heard all of the statements I gave at the beginning of this chapter, in one form or another, particularly the ones that lean heavily on family traditions of no divorce. Unfortunately, "no divorce" often means "no gain, either." This "NGE" factor is the one thing that has characterized most of your behavior in the past, when you were allowing yourself to be trapped by the seven deadly sins, when no action, no risk taking, no change were all part of your daily life.

NGE has to be the bottom line to get you to face the specters of possible separation and possible divorce. If you want your life to continue to remain in the hellish state it is in, then you will quickly and firmly embrace the NGE factor and just hunker in to make the best of it.

The problem with that is twofold: (1) You aren't going to get any better, and (2) neither is the alcoholic. Allowing yourself to remain stuck in neutral with your relationship— with your alcoholic drinking himself to death right under your feet, while you stay just as trapped and just as sick as the alcoholic—is no way to live. The separation or divorce is not going to cure the alcoholism, since there is no cure for the disease. It may not even make you feel a whole lot better, particularly if there are children involved. What *does* it do, then?

It points up the need for treatment to the alcoholic. It says, for the very last time, "I'm *serious* about not sticking around and watching the person I love die from alcohol abuse!" It certainly tells your alcoholic that, finally, some *changes* are going to be made, that he or she is *finally* going to have to choose between you and the bottle! This is something that you may have been threatening for a long time; now you need to face the possibility that all of your threats might just become reality.

Several considerations must be taken into account

when dealing with family traditions of no divorce. It is essential that you help your family understand the nature of the disease that you have been living with and how this disease has affected every aspect of your life with the alcoholic. If there are children involved, help their grandparents understand the ways that your children are being affected by living with an alcoholic parent.

Most families will want to believe that you can work it out or that things'll get better in time. You and I both know that that is Dark Ages thinking and that it isn't going to work. After all, you've tried things like that before. How many times have you given your alcoholic "just one more chance"? Have you been able to keep track of the number of nights that you have sobbed to yourself, "Things'll get better; they *have* to!" only to awaken the next morning and see your alcoholic head downstairs for another little "hair of the dog" to start the day?

Eventually, your parents and the parents or other relatives of the alcoholic need to be informed of what your life has been like, in case they haven't really observed it for themselves.

I think specifically of the cases we have treated where parents of both the alcoholic and the significant-other person lived in different cities. Every time, both sets of parents were convinced that, if the couple just packed up and moved to where the parents lived, the alcohol problem would go away.

This kind of geographic-escape rationale can get so embedded in families that many patients *never* break out of the grip of the alcoholism! They just keep moving around the country, staying with this set of relatives or that set of friends, always looking for just the right spot, where the alcohol problem will go away.

Hopefully, you have come further in your thinking than that. However, I am not discounting for a moment that those parents and other relatives and close friends will need to be dealt with in as firm, polite, loving, and caring a manner as possible.

Traditions are hard things to break; they are some of the very cornerstones that keep people together in the face of many adversities. But there are definitely times when you may have to say, "Tradition be damned! I need to get out!"

One of the toughest roadblocks that you will encounter in arriving at a decision to take steps toward separating will be whatever deep religious ties you may have. I have treated women who have endured intolerable situations at the hands of their alcoholic husbands, whose children have literally begged for a separation or a divorce, yet they refuse to consider such tools because of deep religious convictions. These are generally the same people that turn down almost all tools of a decisive nature, tools that make mandatory actions necessary on their part and on the part of their alcoholic.

Let's set the record straight. I am not saying that you should run right out and file for a separation or a divorce. I am exploring with you the powerful tool that these legal maneuvers are when it seems that other tools have not worked—when the intervention, for example, has failed. Now you are faced with what your biggest consequence was, namely, "If you do not get help, I am leaving you!"

Perhaps no one, you included, ever thought it would come down to this. But you might just be at the point of having to file those papers, and you are *very* frightened. Let's look at that for just a moment. First, you are afraid of the prospect of going through the whole legal process—frightened of lawyers, courts, and judges. Second, you are terrified of the prospect of having your financial base of operations substantially lowered or eliminated. Third, you are petrified at the thought of perhaps spending the rest of your life alone. *Afraid, terrified,* and *petrified* are mighty big buzzwords, aren't they? Just reading them can conjure up the very feelings and emotions that they stand for, and you've felt them all!

Here's what I want you to think about as a counter-move to those fear buzzwords. Think about what your life will continue to be like if you *don't* take some drastic action such as a legal separation. Think about what death from alcoholism will mean both to you and to your children—actually *seeing* someone go through the steadily worsening days and nights of the torture of this disease for who knows how many more months or short years.

Think about what other options are open to you and to your alcoholic. Have you exhausted everything else? Have all other channels to get him or her into treatment been exhausted? What's left for you? What's left for him or her, *without* help?

Finally, think of the love that you have seen being stifled day by day by alcohol abuse, and then think that your getting out of the picture might just be the final act of love that you can bestow on your active alcoholic. Whatever action you might take is not done from a point of hate for the alcoholic; what you *hate* is the disease of alcoholism and what it has done to your lives.

The message that you are going to convey by leaving the relationship is the one that says, "I love you too much to stay here and watch you die at my feet from alcoholism!"

Technically, I am talking about *your* leaving the relationship. We both know that it will be your alcoholic who will be asked to leave the premises, either voluntarily or perhaps through a restraining order obtained by your lawyer. You must never lose sight of the fact that, if you take such a drastic action, it is taken because of your love, care, and concern for the alcoholic, not as a weapon of revenge, hate, havoc-wreaking, or the desire to "ruin" the alcoholic.

You see, even if you tried the intervention that we discussed earlier, and it failed, the consequences are still there for you to use. In fact, you should have put those consequences into force right then if the person refused treatment.

But in the event that you gave in and allowed him to stay so that you could give your alcoholic another chance to do it (quit or "cut down") by himself, you still have the option available to inaugurate your consequences *now*.

Let us assume that you have examined all the pitfalls, have received some counseling, and have determined in spite of everything and everybody that a separation is the only avenue left. Right here and now you should make up your mind that a *legal* separation, in which papers are served upon the alcoholic, is what I'm referring to. You don't have to run right out and file for divorce; that can come later, if it must. But this is one step beyond the one that allows you just to separate temporarily by going home for a while, or to get away from each other for a few weeks.

Those kinds of separations have probably already happened, and you know the results. The alcoholic has stopped or cut down the drinking for the time that you were gone, and then, as soon as you are back together, the disease wins out as it always must, and the alcoholic returns to drinking, harder and longer than ever.

When you take *legal* steps for separation, you still have the option to keep it on hold or cancel it altogether. Just taking that first step of contacting your attorney and getting the paperwork started can be a great deal of help in inspiring your alcoholic to seek treatment.

I can't begin to count all of the couples who've been in our treatment center who got there in the first place because one of the spouses did something more than threaten legal action. It is one of the greatest mini-interventions that can be performed! I call the taking of legal action the "great motivator" because it finally shows the alcoholic partner that you mean business.

It is equally satisfying to see the number of couples who go through the six months of treatment, enter aftercare and A.A. couple's groups and home groups, and do all this *without* ever having to go through the final paperwork for separation or divorce. So many significant-other persons tell me that they intend to keep the paperwork handy, not as a weapon, but as a reminder to both of them how far they had to go to get into treatment and how far they have *come* in their recovery. You can do the same, and that's why I am perhaps forcing you to look at this unpleasant aspect of life with an alcoholic. The idea of using the separation or divorce filing as a mini-intervention means that only you and your immediate relationship are involved. It's sometimes easier for you to handle than a full-scale intervention.

Whatever you decide to do, you will have to go

through what we call the "grief process." Giving up a relationship, even for a short period of time, takes an emotional toll on you in the same fashion that an actual death may affect you. Over and over, I hear patients say, "I'd rather face a death than go through this!" Many of them speak from actual experience; many of them have lost a previous spouse or a parent and found that loss easier to get through than a separation or a divorce.

The steps in the grieving that you will go through will be denial, anger, "candy-boxing," letting go, and acceptance. Some believe that the order of these stages is absolute; I don't think so and have found in actual practice that they can intermix and come and go like a flock of birds around a feeder. Sometimes all of the stages are present, sometimes only one or two. Let's look at them briefly.

Denial

This is an old friend of yours. It is the same tape that has played so often in your past when the uppermost statement that was in your mind was, "This isn't happening; it can't *possibly* be happening to me!" Denial has been assuring you all along that, if you just played the waiting game, everything would turn out OK.

When you are in this stage, your feelings are in a state of shock, of numbness. You tend to mask your real feelings, and you *certainly* don't share what is happening to your relationship with your family, your friends, or neighbors. It's the grand game of hiding your head under the biggest cover of the biggest bed you can find. Maybe, just *maybe*, "I'll wake up and find it's (separation) not really happening!"

Anger

Ah, another old friend! As the time wears on, you allow yourself to feel angry that it has had to come to this. The anger that you have been holding in a kind of inward garbage bag now gets shoved out at everyone in sight.

"Look out! Here's the 'war department' again! Everyone take cover!"

You will probably find yourself raising hell about how bad the other person in your relationship has been. Your anger often gets misplaced, yet it *does* start pouring out.

Candy-Boxing

This is a term I created to describe the stage of grief during which you start bargaining with boxes of candy and bunches of flowers. You are having so many second thoughts that you begin to bargain. You find yourself saying you will change, asking for candy and flowers back from the other person, and looking for a single strand of hope to make it work.

What's happening here is you are really finding it hard to let go of the relationship, so you start this sort of pseudocourting again to see if there is "something there." The danger is, of course, that you are overlooking the alcohol that has prompted all this in the first place!

Letting Go

Here, you enter that part of grieving where depression is likely to rear its ugly head. You are saying goodbye to the relationship, even if temporarily, but at the same time you are wondering what's left in life for you.

This is a stage of grieving where people are inclined to feel suicidal because the relationship they have worked so hard to maintain and build is ending. The depression will pass, and if you understand that, things will get easier. This is also a stage of the grieving process during which good personal inventories can help you find new purposes and new meanings for your life.

This is a tough stage of the grieving process—make no mistake about it—but it is an absolutely necessary part of the whole plan to help you deal with the ending of a relationship.

Acceptance

With this stage of the grief process, you begin to see some light at the end of the tunnel, instead of seeing the headlight of an oncoming train! You will begin to feel some peace with yourself and some freedom from all the pain that you have been experiencing as you have been going through all the other stages.

The most important thing to remember is that you could end up going through some of these stages again if you haven't completely been able to justify filing the separation papers or proceeding with the divorce.

So, keep firmly in mind the fact that you have neither taken these actions lightly nor taken them because you hate the person. That person has a disease, and the disease is to blame for bringing you to this point in your relationship.

You are using this method to point up the seriousness of your intentions to your alcoholic. Your love for him is so strong that you will not allow the relationship to continue in an alcoholic state; therefore, you are contemplating these serious steps.

If your alcoholic understands that you mean business this time, and that you are not merely playing head games with her, there might be a chance for this ploy to work in the intervention vein in which it is being presented here.

A word of caution: It doesn't always work! The alcoholic can let you go right ahead and file the papers and order him out of the house or let you leave the residence. It doesn't matter if he is at such a stage that he is willing to continue to choose the bottle over the baby.

Alcoholics will want to agree to enter treatment or marriage counseling without dealing with the alcohol problem, except on a superficial basis. They will think that once you have entered treatment together, there will be no reason for you to keep the legal actions going. They are crafty and sly creatures, and you will need to remain on guard so that you are not lulled into thinking that things are changing, when in fact they are merely being put on hold, mostly to pacify you!

Separation and divorce are not pretty solutions to the problems of an alcoholic relationship. They are tools, however, that will need to be in your arsenal for wellness, if *all* other means to treatment, and hence recovery processes, have been exhausted. Treat them as loaded and dangerous weapons—with respect and with caution!

Part IV
THE BRIGHT FUTURE

17

Getting Well Together

"It's raining cats and dogs out there! Whaddaya mean we're gonna have a picnic?"

"Go to Mexico? Hell, Beth, we can't even afford to go to your mother's for the weekend!"

"The zoo? You gotta be kidding! That's for kids!"

Ah, yes! The familiar strains of the "Couples Overture" as played in countless homes, apartments, and condos weekend after weekend, all across America! These couples are trying in vain to do something together that might be fun, and they have no idea how to get going, particularly because the familiar six-pack or two of beer or the bottle of California red are no longer available as real party starters. What to do?

For the couple in recovery, there *is* a bright future, but you have to work at it! Heck, throughout this entire book we've been talking about the value of taking risks, of doing some really hard work in the areas of changing your lives to live them joyfully without alcohol. So this chapter and the remaining ones in this section of the book won't be any easier on you! I want you to do some more hard work for the reward of getting well together. But this kind of work, this getting well together, is a wonderful experience that couples are enjoying week after week in recovery. I know because we see them and work with them at the Gateway Treatment Center, and we can see the results.

Take Sarah and Sam as examples. They have discovered the joy of heading up to the mountains in their camper for a day of fishing, except now there's no six-pack in the front seat to start an argument or three. Now they actually put a line in the stream! Sam told my couple's group, "If you'd told me six months ago I could have spent the day actually *fishing*, without two or three six-packs, I would have said you're nuts!"

And Sarah added, "Sam never even let me get near the fishing gear before, even though I'm as good at it as he is! *My* only function on these trips was to keep fetching another 'tall boy'!"

This couple has learned the beauty of getting well together, and their enthusiasm is infectious. Other couples share with us the experience of going to a ball game and actually *seeing* the game for a change. Football and beer has been replaced by football and *fun*, for the first time in their lives, now that alcohol has completely left their relationship.

In *The Joy of Being Sober*, I spent almost all the pages showing readers how the recovering person makes changes to learn to live productively without alcohol. My first book is exactly that: a descriptive book that is intended to help readers replace sadness at giving up the best friend of alcohol with the joy of a newfound friend in the form of life without chemical interference.

For you, the recovering couple, there is just as much undiscovered new country out there, waiting for your prospecting, waiting for your own revelations about the joys that life has to offer you, all in the process of getting well together. And it's fun!

A good example is the old standby, the rainy day picnic.

The Rainy Day Picnic

Imagine that it's the first weekend the two of you have been able to plan together for some time. Your alcoholic has reluctantly agreed to try a picnic, and you have begun to feel some childish enthusiasm yourself, reliving memories of times when picnics were grand and glorious things to you.

Your recovering alcoholic is pretty skittish about the

whole thing for an obvious reason. Picnics have meant just one thing to him: "Where's the kegger going to be, and what time should we be there?" But there isn't going to be a keg or even a single can on *this* picnic, so you haven't been getting as much enthusiasm as you might have wanted. Don't worry; it'll come!

At any rate, there you are, putting the lunch into the hamper, when the rain clouds that have been threatening really break out. It's *definitely* going to rain on your parade! What to do? Well, you shift your thinking from bright sunshine and lush green grass to cozy living room, den, or even kitchen floor!

"We're gonna have our picnic *where?*" he says, not quite believing what he's just heard.

"I said, we're still going to have a picnic—right *here*, so turn on the radio and help me spread the blanket on the floor."

You can do it! Have a rainy day picnic right at home. Sure, there will be some obvious differences. For one, the ever-present picnic ants won't be around to get their share of crumbs, but you probably won't mind that a lot! The point is simply to re-create the mood of the picnic that you had originally planned for the great outdoors. For instance, I mentioned a *radio* above, not a *stereo*, because you'd hardly take your stereo components along on a picnic. If, like me, you like to listen to music at picnics, simulate the real thing by using a portable instead of simply flipping on the family stereo system. Likewise, if you were going to pack a thermos of coffee, cocoa, or iced tea, go ahead and do it. Don't just bring in the coffeepot, as you would at any meal at home.

You are going to have a lot of fun, believe it or not, getting you both into the spirit of going ahead and having your picnic, despite the weather. Spread out your blanket or your inexpensive red-and-white checkered picnic tablecloth and have your picnic right there in the favorite room of your house.

Were you going to build a campfire and cook some hot dogs? Well, build a small fire in your fireplace, if you have one. If you don't, take the little hibachi you usually

use at picnics and set it out on the patio or front porch.
Such a portable grill costs only about $10 at discount
stores, and you can always cover it, just as you would if a
sudden summer rain came up when you were on a real
outdoor picnic.

Go ahead and do *everything* just the way you had
planned! It's a riot to hear folks describe all the new
problems that their rainy day picnic offered them, and it's
even more fun to hear how they solved them. I think of
one couple in particular who were unpacking the hamper
on the floor in front of their fireplace. They had just gotten
a fire going, one that was just enough to take the chill "out
of the air." As the woman was taking out the sandwiches
and the tub of potato salad, she noticed that she had
forgotten to pack the saltshaker. Well, she said what any
of you might say under similar circumstances: "Be right
back—I forgot the salt!"

"Hold it!" her companion said. "This is supposed to
be a picnic! We wouldn't be jumping up and heading
home for the salt! Let's just wing it *without* the salt." And
they did!

The whole point is that they carried out their picnic
plan, ate their lunch without the missing salt, and enjoyed
it immensely. They went along with the *idea* of being on a
picnic, and they had fun!

Time is another factor you should consider for authen-
ticity. If it was going to be an afternoon of at least four
hours, stick to that plan. Just because you're home, don't
fudge on the time you two had set aside for yourselves. If
you had planned to take along a book, or perhaps the
Sunday papers to read after eating, then do so! Pack up
your stuff in the hamper, pour yourself another cup of
cocoa or coffee, turn over on your tummy, and start reading.

Kids involved? Fine. Let them play whatever games
they can still play, despite the weather, including whatever kind of board game or toy they would have taken
along to use at the park or beach or mountain.

You will definitely have to fight the desire just to quit
your picnic and get on with some dumb household chore
like cleaning or laundry. That's not fair! You planned a

picnic, so have one. No fair using tables or good plates, either! Set your picnic on the "ground" just as you would outside. Use paper plates, or maybe those special wicker things that make the paper plates more stable, and forget the silver! Use the same gear from your picnic hamper that you always use, because that's part of the fun!

If you have taken the family pet on your outings before, then do so today as well. I guarantee that all of you will have a wonderful time *just being together* on your rainy day picnic. And no one will miss the booze!

Coffee Table Tripping

What about exotic trips, like the trip to Mexico mentioned in the beginning of this chapter? Well, you can have them! Of course, you are really going to have to do more planning than going, and I realize that is going to fall short of the mark for many of you. However, it is the togetherness that I am urging you to try, the wellness that can be generated by planning the dream trip both of you would like to take.

Here's how it works. For several weeks ahead of a designated trip-planning day, you go out separately to gather travel brochures and folders on places each of you would like to visit, from travel agents, the airport, or perhaps through the mails. It costs you nothing but some of your time, which is a bargain when you consider the romantic evening your trip-planning day can lead to.

Together, you sit down on the floor by the coffee table. (I am big on sitting on the floor because it brings you closer together and prevents either of you from being in a dominant position over the other.) You have taken the time to put the names of the proposed destinations in a jar, and a random drawing determines which city or country you two will look at this evening.

Let's say it is New York City. Whoever has been collecting all the folders that pertain to the Big Apple starts laying things out on the table. Colorful brochures show the million things to do in that city, the current theater fare, the restaurants, and of course the shopping!

Now, shopping is an important part of your trip. You may have gathered up a Sunday *New York Times* and pulled the zillion Sunday supplements from it, the wonderful ads for the exotic to the everyday. Before you know it, you two are literally lost in the magic of your trip to New York City!

You'll need a large pad of paper if you're going to do this right. Head it "Budget for Our Trip to New York," and begin to list the cost of transportation and hotels, spending money, etc. You will have to do a good deal of estimating, but it will be fun scouring the literature to get close enough to know what you should be setting aside for this trip.

Many people have told me that the hours just seemed to fly by during such "coffee table tripping" between a recovering alcoholic and the significant other. It is an endless source of great fun, but it also has a very practical side. It allows both of you to plan, budget, and begin to realize the possibility of making such a trip. If the alcoholic in your life is willing to set aside just the amount of money that was being spent on liquor for your trip budget, you'll be on your way to the place of your dreams before you know it!

If you approach your coffee table tripping with an open mind, you'll soon realize that your options are endless and that doing the research is half the fun. Set your imagination to work and consider "bed and breakfast" vacations, bicycle touring, or backpacking your way around a foreign country.

A big bonus of this planning is that you will begin to see that something you might always have dreamed about can happen! If you take a step beyond getting the alcoholic to agree to commit the drinking funds of the past to your trip and open a separate bank account, the possibility of actually taking the trip will seem even more real. A savings account will reward you with interest, and if you can afford to put away a little more than the old drinking money, it will build your trip fund very quickly. Once again, the payoff for you both is being together, planning something together, and having fun getting well together!

Once you have the needed funds, you'll be able to take the trip, and then it's back to the coffee table to assemble a photo album of your treasures! You wait a couple of months and then start the coffee table tripping all over again, drawing the name of another city or country from your dream jar. I must confess that I try to slip a favorite city back into the jar, if I want to work on it again. I'm willing to let the luck of the draw work for me! You two can do the same. Over and over, in spite of how silly it sounds, I have insisted that couples try this coffee table tripping, and they have never been sorry.

There are many variations on the planning routine, depending on your desires and resources. If you like to stick to nearer horizons and take short automobile or RV trips, you might want to take into account other variables when stocking your dream jar. For example, your jar could be stuffed with the number, kinds, and locations of specialized campgrounds, along with things to do and places to see.

Steamship cruises, flying and sailing trips, ski or scuba diving trips, "Windjammer" cruises, even trips built around running, parasailing, or amateur photography and archaeology are great candidates for coffee table tripping. When you try this and it works out for you, will you drop me a line in care of my publisher and tell me about it? I'd love to share your experience with other recovering couples on the wellness trail.

Local Jaunts

I mentioned the zoo, didn't I? Did you think that was utterly absurd? Well, maybe! But if you simply discard the idea, you and your recovering person are going to miss out on a great afternoon or so. When is the last time you went to the zoo or animal park *without* kids?

Just the two of you strolling hand in hand through the many wonders of the zoo, getting all messed up with cotton candy or ice-cream-on-a-stick, is a delight that should *not* be spent on just the younger people in your life! I call this event "two-zooing," and it's an absolute blast for all ages of twosomes! Grab any old camera so you record how happy the two of you look when you are engaging in an activity that does not involve alcohol.

You may want to combine this sort of day with a picnic that really happens in the outdoors. That's great, but don't hinge one on the other, since both events can stand as worthwhile experiences on their own and you can certainly get a full day of togetherness out of either of these things.

If you don't have a zoo handy, do you have a museum? They're not musty old places anymore, you know! You've spent hours and hours in a foul-smelling bar, cocktail lounge, or other drinking establishment, but have some great dread about stepping foot inside a wonderful museum! Art or antiquity, it doesn't matter. You probably won't be allowed to do the cotton candy and ice cream bit, but you certainly can have lunch in many a fine museum.

You may not have such a place in the town where you live. No problem. There must be a museum of some kind or another within driving distance of where you live. You can even do a little coffee table tripping to find out the closest and most interesting such places, something you might do round-trip in one day by car. That way you can get an added pleasure from two togetherness events: trip planning and the museum itself.

Doing any of these things in a state of sobriety is such an incredibly different and exhilarating experience that you really have to trust me and try it for yourself! Alcoholics need to be introduced in the sobriety stage to those things they never would have dreamed of doing while in the active drinking stages of the disease. There is no comparison.

Dancing

One of the things that comes up among our patients frequently is the notion that dancing is a thing of the past, because "I can never dance without a drink or two!" Well, that's just plain hogwash! A lady recently said to me, "Do you have any idea how wonderful it is to dance with someone who has not been drinking?"

"Sure," was the reply. "Do *you* know how wonderful it is to *be able* to dance without drinking?"

It's all in the way you look at things. It's all in the way you begin to take risks and examine what your life can be like without alcohol. I've already introduced you to *The Joy of Being Sober*, my book for recovering alcoholics and those who love them. In those pages you will find other ideas that have proven to be workable and successful as new tools and methods for living a wonderful life without alcohol.

The rainy day picnics, coffee table tripping, and two-zooing discussed in this chapter are just examples of the activities that are part of the process of getting well together. Home for you has not been a very happy place in the past, and the new things you do at home will make you see the place you live with your alcoholic in a new and better light. The things you do away from home, but do *together*, will cast a new and softer, more loving glow on your relationship. That's what life is all about, isn't it?

If you have made it this far into the bright future that lies ahead for you and your alcoholic, then you are going to go all the way! These times are just the base of the mountain that you two can climb together, if you make the effort, and if you are willing to take the risks involved. Don't delay! There's rain in today's forecast, the living room floor is ant-free, and your picnic's waiting!

18

Improving Communications

Have you ever had the feeling that the two of you are strangers? You know, you are sitting there on the couch, watching television, and you sneak a side glance at your now recovering mate. Who is that person? Oh, the physical characteristics remain the same, except things *look* better now that alcohol is out of the way. But wait! There's definitely something different.

And then it hits you; you suddenly feel as if you don't know this person sitting next to you. During all the weeks, months, or years that you have been living with and loving an alcoholic, you have had the reactions, the feelings, the emotions, and the angers that have been centered around someone you love using a chemical substance to live with you! And now that chemical is gone. What in the world are the two of you going to do with each other?

We have been exploring some new tools for you to use, some practical kinds of field trips into the world of the sober, but now we are going to have to look at perhaps the toughest new assignment of them all: how are you going to learn to *communicate*?

You *are* two different people; make no mistake about that. When people come into treatment with me I always tell them that many times a couple will not survive recovery. That's not a very pleasant thing to hear, but it's the truth. The two people who enter treatment with alcohol as the focus of their lives are going to end treatment as two new folks, *both* of whom are in recovery from the ravages of the disease. Once again, it's downright scary. You knew how to deal with the alcoholic who was drinking actively. You had a handle on exactly what game plan would have to be used in order to get through whatever might turn up as a result of the drinking.

But now you don't have alcohol to blame for those awkward periods of silence between the two of you. When we talked about using the ten-minute drill or the rainy day picnic, I already knew that the most difficult of all assignments was awaiting you. How do you ever learn to talk with one another while sober?

Well, scary or not, let's wade in! To start, put a real positive stroke in your life by saying, "This is going to be *exciting* for us!"

And it will. Trust me! The material that we'll look at together is the basis of the lecture that my partner Paul has used for many years when he talks to our patients about communications. What I have done is adapt some of these basics to address you specifically, the significant other, and I have given the levels of communication different titles from those that Paul uses, again, to speak directly to you as opposed to speaking to your recovering alcoholic.

With that in mind, and with credit duly given to Paul, let's look at the five levels of communication that you are presently capable of working in. These are:

1. the "what's for dinner?" opening
2. the "have you heard what Myrna said?" gambit
3. the "weather forecast/wear your galoshes" order
4. the "I *feel* this way about *that*" opening
5. the "Concerto for you and me"

You and your recovering person probably spend most of your time using these five levels of communication to "talk" with each other. I use quotation marks around *talk* because talk is basically conversation without feeling. Communicating is expressing gut-level feelings with words, actions, and counterwords and counteractions. There *is* a difference!

An important point about this list is that the forms of

communication are listed in ascending order of desirability and difficulty. Now that you know that, reverse the order of the entire list, so that number 5 becomes number 1 and so on.

1. the "Concerto for you and me"
2. the "I *feel* this way about *that*" opening
3. the "weather forecast/wear your galoshes" order
4. the "have you heard what Myrna said?" gambit
5. the "what's for dinner?" opening

The reason for this is that I want you to value the first level, the "Concerto for you and me," as the most perfect level of communications, the one in which perfect harmony is being achieved by the two of you. This is the *ultimate* in communication skills and hence is the most difficult to achieve.

Most likely, you can readily see that through most of your life with your alcoholic—and perhaps with many other people in your life—you have been talking through the other four levels, and probably spending a large percentage of your time in levels five, four, and three. Let's look at them one at a time in the original ascending order. I think you'll probably recognize these as your own methods of communication in the past.

The "What's for Dinner?" Opening

How many times has your alcoholic, male or female, come tearing through the front door and begun a "conversation" with that phrase? It has been the butt of countless thousands of cartoons, party gags, what have you. Your response to the line has traditionally been, "Can't you even say hello first?"

Just think about it! That kind of exchange has constituted the bulk of the conversations between the two of you. That's pretty funny in itself, and yet millions of you are out there doing it every day and night, thinking that you are having a "conversation." It's sad!

You may now be able to see that the reason you

remain stuck there in that level five communication is that *there are no risks involved*. No one is taking a chance, unless of course the answer to what you are preparing for dinner elicits an argument like "Meat loaf *again?*"

What I am referring to is a different kind of risk—an emotional one. There are no emotional or feeling risks involved in level five talk. It doesn't even have the rank of "small talk" or the gossip level we will look at next. It's just totally safe, dull, boring jargon that is not even thought about very carefully before being said. It just sort of automatically creeps out of your mouth or your alcoholic's as easily as others might say, "Hi, I'm home!" Incidentally, the latter statement, while possibly more genial, is another example of this level of communication. You can run through your entire repertoire of level five statements and see that these are the kinds of "talking" that you and your alcoholic have been engaging in for a long time. You need to shoot for a better level!

The "Have You Heard What Myrna Said?" Gambit

Believe it or not, at this level you are moving more toward feeling, and that's what you and I are aiming for. In this category, though, you're still evading the issue. You've gone beyond the pragmatic "What's for dinner" level, so you probably think you're doing some serious communicating when you gossip.

Well, you *are* getting into a little bit of feelings work, but it is all based on rumors that trigger emotions concerning someone else ("poor old Myrna"). You think you're making an effort to communicate, but you turn to the subject of other people because it's completely *safe* to discuss them. Be honest! How many times have you grasped at the smallest piece of news or gossip to give the appearance of communicating while avoiding that frightening topic of yourselves?

The worst part of being stuck at this level is that, if

you don't have any "reliable" gossip, you'll **invent** some, just to be able to talk about something with your alcoholic!

When the two of you become so comfortable in using this level of communication, you think that you are really talking to each other, totally unaware that you aren't talking *to* each other at all, but are talking *about* someone else. When you stop and look at it, you can see that it applies even to the kinds of things you may tell each other about your own children.

"Do you know what Amy said today?" becomes a form of gossipy communication and doesn't tax either you or your partner to do any more than "chew on" whatever little tidbit of news you are passing along. It's too sad to be funny, but as a significant other you should be squirming in your chair right now, realizing how many times you have fallen, nay *led* yourself, into this level four communication web!

The "Weather Forecast/Wear Your Galoshes" Order

This third level of communication is one that doesn't even require much work on your part, so you use it a heck of a lot! Here, locked firmly into this level, you simply exchange a bunch of facts, passing it off as communication.

Paul calls this the "facts and judgments" level. You can see how it applies to you, a significant other. You shoot out a statement that really doesn't have a lot of opportunity for comeback, issue an "executive order" to go with the statement, and then sit back and expect someone to quarrel with this order!

It's an equally safe level from which to operate. It doesn't require a whole lot of skill and really fits the caretaker/enabler part of your personality that simply issues facts and solutions about things, not leaving a whole lot of room for choice on the part of your recovering person. You'd absolutely be thrown a wicked curve if there were any deviation from this level. Suppose the alcoholic comes back with a statement that *contradicts* yours. Oh, boy! Now we've got "trouble in River City," as Meredith Willson's *Music Man* cast might sing.

If your recovering person dares to advance an idea that it might *not* rain, and that therefore he or she is *not* going to take galoshes, then your orders are being ignored or violated, and you are liable to lose your cool, have a big fight, and then complain, "We don't *communicate* anymore!"

When your alcoholic was drinking, you did so many of those enabling things automatically that it has never occurred to you that the recovering person might be able to make some decisions on his own. Responses like "Doesn't look much like rain to me. I'll take my galoshes, but don't believe I need to wear 'em," can throw your whole level three game plan into chaos. So watch it! When you are making level three statements, try working for a better level of communications. Try saying things like, "Did you hear the forecast this morning? I thought it said we should expect rain today. What did *you* hear?"

Now we are working toward communicating! We are having you express a thought about a statement (it might rain) and are seeking a response as to the other person's *interpretation* of what was being said, subsequently arriving at a *joint* decision (to take or wear the galoshes) based on this joint receiving of information. You are allowing for the other person's ability to process essential information for himself, hence making a rational decision and taking some responsibility for himself.

The "I *Feel* This Way About *That*" Opening

This "I statement" opening is one of the toughest for you as a significant other to learn to use, but it is absolutely essential if you are ever to get on a feeling level and *stay* there in your new life of recovery and sobriety together.

What it demands is that you communicate on the basis of how *you* are feeling about something and, by expressing truly how *you* feel, hope to draw out the feelings of the person with whom you are talking. Here, your exact wording and tone of voice are all-important to convey an open expression of *your* feelings alone. For example, you might say, "I'm feeling angry about the way you treated me last night!"

So far so good. That's a simple statement about *how* you feel. You must be careful about how you phrase your follow-up: "I wonder if you can *help* me with *why* I'm feeling that way?"

You see, you are not condemning the other person or putting him on the defensive; you are merely asking for some *validation* for the reason that you are feeling angry. The person of whom you ask such a favor will usually process quickly what he might have said or done to contribute to your anger. It is hoped that he will then *verbalize* those actions to you, which will make him realize what has caused you to feel the way you do. When that realization happens, the two of you are beginning to deal with each other on a *feeling* level, and that's the very best kind!

At this level of communication, we are, however, dealing with only *one* set of feelings: *yours*. This makes it a difficult level for you to reach because you are not used to being able to express how you feel without asking for big trouble from your actively drinking alcoholic.

With recovery and sobriety, you will learn to become skilled in expressing how you really feel. An overworked statement that is always connected with therapists says, "It's important for you to get in touch with your feelings!" As hackneyed as that may sound, it's accurate.

We all have feelings, but as a significant other, you have learned that you have often buried those feelings. When you did that, you didn't deal with them at all; you just let them sit there, moldering into bitter resentments that are very hard to deal with now.

Remember that the key to level two communications is always to state the way *you* are feeling about a particular event, thing, person. Mostly, this will focus on the emotions you find cropping up between the two of you.

This level two communication can be seen as a one-two punch. First you state *how* you feel; then you *ask for help* with what's making you feel that way. It's guaranteed to work, the more you use it and the more comfortable you are with it.

When I hear about patients' success with the tools I've offered them, I always ask them what made them decide to take the risk. They invariably say, "Nothing else was working, so I decided to try this way and see what would happen. When it worked, I nearly shouted and fell off my chair! It was *so* simple!" So simple, and yet so hard for the significant other to try.

The whole concept of feeling levels of communications is like a foreign language to you, and it's understandable if the phrases sound stilted to you. They *are* stilted because they're intended to convey your interest in taking the first step of expressing your feelings without provoking the defensive response that your condemnations of the past have invariably caused. If you simply can't bring yourself to use the wording I've given, rephrase your statements to make you more comfortable with them, as long as you stick to the general idea.

The point is that you need to move off those barricades that have kept you from knowing each other on this new level. If the recovering alcoholic responds to your request for help in understanding the feelings you've expressed, she will get a clue as to how *she* has been acting. Thus, improved communications begin to happen.

The "Concerto for You and Me"

Well, we finally arrive at the *best and hardest* level. This is the *numero uno*, the payoff. And it's a toughie! What makes this level so difficult lies in the fact that it is a state of perfect harmony with each other. Like a symphony playing, this "Concerto for You and Me" is the one we are all striving for in the fine art of communications.

It distinguishes itself from all others because it truly hinges on the success of being able to share feelings—deep, emotional, gut wrenching feelings—but doing it together. Paul Staley calls this the "peak" level; it's hard to climb! What makes it worthwhile is that the couple does it as a twosome, instead of just one of them having the courage to share feelings.

This ability to give and take on a purely feeling level is what you should be striving for to improve your communications. It is only possible if neither of you is offended by what is said, if there is a true, sincere desire to allow the expression of feelings, without feeling threatened by what is said.

Of course it's tough to do! But it is at this level of communications that a couple truly realize all that being in perfect harmony with each other means. It is in the constant playing of this "Concerto for Two" that you and your alcoholic come out of the Dark Ages of the previous early stages of communications and climb to the *peak* level.

Things that were *never* discussed or had too many taboos to be discussed can now be shared in an intimacy of understanding and respect for how the other party feels and for what steps can be taken to *keep* the feeling channel open for more complete love, understanding, and resolving of conflict between the two of you.

So there we have the five levels of communication as I see them applying to you, the significant other, loving an alcoholic! The last point of "conflict resolution" that I just wrote about, is one that is so prevalent in all relationships that it can only effectively be dealt with when you understand and strive to improve your particular levels.

If a therapist can get you both to understand how poorly you have used any tools within your grasp to resolve conflicts, he or she will certainly have attained high marks! When you and your alcoholic begin to see that you must move beyond the cliche and gossip levels and plunge deep into the feeling levels of communication, you will be on your way to having the power within the relationship to resolve conflicts that have been there for a long time.

In all that you do as a couple, improving your communications is one of the most important. You have the capability to make things better in your life together, if you will simply do three things:

*   *   *

1. Look at *how* (at what level) you talk together now.
2. Look at *what* has made you afraid to share feelings (his/her possible relapse?).
3. Look at *what* level you want to achieve and *where*, *how*, and *when* you want to start.

The orchestra awaits your downbeat! It's up to you to make the first move, a move that can lead you to better stages of communication for a lifetime.

19

Looking at Your New Relationship

What's it like? How is it feeling to you? You now have a new relationship in which you are actually talking to each other as opposed to waging armed hostilities, in which you actually *care* about how the other person feels.

It's kind of like a new pair of shoes, isn't it? There's a sense of pride in owning the latest fashion, but it still might *pinch* a little when you walk! It all seems possible, and even *that* is pretty scary. For such a long time you just kept listening to all your old tapes and pretty well convinced yourself that you were doomed to a half-life with an alcoholic.

But that's over now! You're on the road to using some new tools, learning some new ways to live to keep on *loving* an alcoholic. We've run some new ideas up the flagpole. Did you salute? Have there been some things that you have read so far that turned on a few "action buttons" for you? I hope so! I'm certainly going to assume that you are still open to some other ideas to keep your new relationship looking as bright and shiny as a new car.

It will still take work. I don't know of any plan that has ever been advanced that doesn't require effort on your part. It certainly requires that you and your alcoholic look at the new ways of doing things with an eye toward improving the quality of your life together in recovery.

With that in mind, suppose you begin a journey of imagination into the coming weeks and months—hopefully years—that you and your alcoholic can mature together in a warm and lasting relationship. You're going to learn to be *selfish*.

You, the significant other, "in order to form a more perfect union," hereby pledge to *begin doing some things for yourself*. I mean the sort of activities that may have rattled around in your mind for years but have never been allowed to come very strongly to the surface. These could be going back to school, taking up a new hobby or craft, making a career change, or getting your first full-time job.

Any and every sort of imaginable dream must now be allowed to come forth for examination *by the two of you*, as a potential for increasing the excitement in your new life. I don't mean to imply that your life has been dull and boring up to this point; I only want to point out that *most* of your effort has been applied to dealing with the drinking problem alone.

Recovery allows you to expand your thinking and your universe. It gives you the clear pathway to say, "I'll do something for myself, something that will make me feel *good* again." When you are thinking like this, you can only add to the value of your new relationship.

I keep saying *new* relationship, because that's what it is. The two of you feel reborn into this complicated but exciting business of living, and it's going to be just damn fine! The way you are going to get comfortable with actually *living* your lie instead of just *existing* is to take some more risks. You thought you were off the hook with that one, I know. But risk taking and the business of making changes are so important to a life that is free from the bondage of alcoholism that I can't stress them enough!

You might just want to go back to a school and take one course in something you've always wanted to learn. That's great! You don't need to be enrolled in a degree program unless that's something that you've really wanted to do. It would be good enough just for you to be able to "selfishly" take those few hours a week to get back in the swim of learning something new again.

This can revitalize your life, charge the batteries that you have allowed to drain, at the same time providing new material for bonding between you and your recovering person. I use this "go for the brass rings" concept so much that people are always giving me brass objects for my desk or home!

But I believe it to be an essential part of the way your new relationship will be nurtured. When you have the security of knowing that what you will do for yourself is in no way a *threatening* move to the relationship, it will be all the more sweet!

If your "brass ring" is going back to school, go for it! If you have wanted to take ballet (even at your age), then, for heaven's sake, get started in a class! Has the "Jane Fonda workout" finally convinced you to try a few sessions of aerobics or jazzercise? It's *your* aching body, so go ahead and take the plunge! What about the art lessons you have always known you wanted? There are plenty of *free* instruction settings available through community centers and service organizations. Maybe you have wanted to learn some carpentry or creative cooking. There *are* avenues in your community for exploring those things. All you have to do is seek them out!

Why is it so important to go out and get involved in something new? Because of its value to the relationship, which has suffered from lack of nurturing.

Certainly, you have had something to give your alcoholic, and he or she has had something to give back to you. But think of the relationship as a product of the two of you, as a distinct entity that requires something from each of you, like a child that takes from each of its parents. When you are "selfishly" involved in something that is *doing something for you*, you will be contributing something to the relationship as well. You will become a more interesting person, someone who is worthy of himself or herself. When your own self-esteem rises because of what you are accomplishing, the relationship begins to swell also!

You, in doing something to raise your own self-esteem, begin to demonstrate that you have a new value in this relationship and that it must be reckoned with by your recovering person. When you are involved in something that is just for you, you take on a new dimension for the person who has been assuming that you don't care about yourself, where you go, or what you accomplish.

That's sad! When you have stood in front of the mirror in the morning after showering or shaving, have you liked what you have seen? Have you been able to hold your head high and face the world out there? Or has it been such a down and depressing life that you can hardly look yourself in the eye?

Going for the brass rings of your life does something especially wonderful; it gives you a sense of *value* about who you are and what you are, not only to the one you love, but also to yourself! Self-love, or self-respect, is not vanity. Rather, it is a strong asset that will help your new relationship grow stronger and stronger.

Before, in the active drinking stage, you had very little self-respect. You were locked into playing all your old tapes of the seven deadly sins, weren't you? It was playing those old tapes that kept you locked in your own prison. After all, no one expects anything out of someone like you, forever muddling around on the rim of the "pity pot" and desperately *hoping* you might fall in!

Now that all of that is past, you need to seek the other outlets that are all around you, outlets that can help build your self-confidence and your self-respect. Just like your alcoholic, you will need to avoid making *drastic* changes in your life for the first six months of recovery.

For example, you are not suddenly going to chuck your high-paying job and go to school full-time unless you are named an heir to a large family fortune! No, you will need to temper all of your actions with such mundane things as available money, time, and resources to meet the everyday requirements of your life. In other words, it obviously makes no sense for you to have to bring in a full-time governess just so you can go to college full-time! That would only exacerbate some already strained feelings between you and your alcoholic.

What it *can* mean, though, is that you can afford to get someone to come in for a few hours a week to allow your recharging of emotional batteries. When you are at home with your alcoholic, you will have new fuel for your conversation, new worlds that you can share as you move toward the higher levels of communication.

The playing of an instrument, the painting of a picture, or the serving of a gourmet meal will provide hours and hours of new relationship talk for you and your recovering person. So, the so-called "selfish" things that you need to consider doing are really designed to make the relationship experience nurturing and growth.

Has the poem you have written today been met with appreciation more than the gift to which it was attached? How have you felt about yourself? Have you been facing each new day with the excitement of what you might be able to do for yourself this day and hence do for the relationship? When you begin to make the changes in your own life, you also begin to make changes in the life of the relationship.

What about making a *major* move? Is this a good idea? It might be, but one of the things that you will have to weigh is where you will get the support that you both need. That support must continue to solidify not only sobriety, but the new relationship as well. The answer is obvious: The fellowship of A.A. and Al-Anon is there for you, wherever you go!

What you may have to do is be a pioneer. It may be up to you and your recovering person to get a recovering couple's group together in the new city or town where you move. Obviously, there are many things to be considered, but generally, your recovering person will make some new friends through the fellowship, and before you know it, you'll probably meet some new couples!

If geographic changes can be avoided in the first six months after you and your alcoholic have completed treatment, I suggest that you adhere to that plan. It is a very big thing to pack up and move across the country, and the stress and anxiety levels get very high for the newly recovered, not to mention the stress and strain that *you* will have to endure.

However, I realize that many times a company or job opportunity presents itself, and there really is no choice but to pull up stakes and start off somewhere new. While this will put a strain on things, you can keep all the tools of the relationship, all the communications skills you have hopefully been using, and make the move with as little emotional disruption as possible.

If a move is absolutely necessary, you should make it together, not with one of you heading off alone to take the responsibility of choosing a place to live, etc. Many times, of course, that isn't possible, but then you need to look at making as exciting an adventure as possible out of the situation. Perhaps the two of you can spend a couple of weekends at the new site, scouting possible home locations or temporary quarters. In other words, if you have to make a move, make the most of it by staying *together*.

There is a strong tendency for couples literally to throw down the tools they have learned when things don't go fast enough for them in recovery. You will need to practice patience, over and over again, reminding yourselves that you have spent a long time being sick together; you need to spend a little more time getting *well* together!

Don't ever think that the alcohol problem is going to be left behind in the city that you leave! That's very dangerous and needs to be guarded against. You will be under even more pressures going to a new place, making new friends, and finding the right places to shop, live, and raise any children that you may have. The temptation for your alcoholic to think that he or she may have suddenly left the alcohol problem in the old place and that, therefore, it will be OK to have a drink or two, is very great!

A new town, a new start, represents an opportunity to slip back into a relapse, and you will have to be on your guard for the telltale signs of the BUD, as well as the new pressures that will come to the surface with the move from one city to another. But if you *must* go, do it with an attitude of reaching for another brass ring.

Here's a good place to discuss the ten-minute drill that I have suggested to you from time to time in this book. Here I will go into it in more detail because it is the perfect tool for your new relationship. Use it as a method for *you* to take some new risks in the areas of simple expression of your own feelings about a particular subject of controversy.

First, let's look at the game rules for using the ten-minute drill. People have asked me to revise these rules every so often because of something they have discovered that has really worked for them. Most often, they suggest that a specific time of day and/or day of the week should be set for the drill.

Well, if that works for you, OK. My experience indicates that there is really no limit to when you can drill. What is important is the fact that you *should* drill when you feel that something is really stuck in your craw. If, say, Saturday morning when the kids are watching cartoons, immersed in nine different cereals all over the den floor, is the only time that you and your recovering person have to resolve conflict or to use the drill as a means of self-expression, do it then!

I would prefer that you follow the basic rules for the ten-minute drill, which suggest there be *no* kids, pets, or others around for the time you are drilling. Do what you have to do, but do it! Here we go.

First of all, you need some sort of timing device that lets you know when ten minutes have elapsed. I suggest the timer that's on most ranges/ovens. A cake mixer of the deluxe category was suggested to me as a great timer because it has a bell that will let you know when the ten minutes have expired. At any rate, some sort of device that makes a sound when ten minutes are used is necessary. This ten-minute period tells both participants that the initial drill is over. You have permission to ask each other whether you feel OK to drill for another ten minutes or whether emotions have gotten to such a peak that you should agree to quit.

At the end of the time period, the party who has brought up the drill in the first place, and may have been doing most of the talking, needs to ask his partner how she is feeling at this point.

"Do you feel OK to continue this discussion for another ten minutes?" he asks.

If the reply is affirmative, then you reset the timing

device for another ten-minute segment. You continue in this fashion until there has been a satisfactory resolution or until either party determines that the emotional level has reached too high a peak to continue.

This is an important part of the basic rules for the drill. If one party or the other, at the conclusion of the ten-minute segment, feels too angry or "slugged over the head" verbally, then he or she has the right to call time out. Use the hand signal that the quarterback uses (the right extended palm crossed on top of the left hand) and say, "Time out! I'm too angry to continue. Let's put it on hold for a while."

"OK," you reply, "but when will you agree to talk this over again?"

Here we have another basic rule. No point of discussion can get buried permanently without resolution. You can call time out and state the reason you can't continue, but you *must* agree to do another drill at another time. You must also make it your responsibility to see that the drill *does* happen.

When any drill takes place, there can be (if you really follow the basic rules) *no stereo, TV, telephone, or doorbell* interruption for the period of the drill. Take the phone off the hook if you have to; make sure not even the family dog is nestled at your feet to provide any disturbance or straying of attention from each other.

The drill is *not* an open fight! It is a tool to allow you to resolve a point of discussion, to allow you to express your feelings about a particular topic that has become a barrier in your relationship. You arrive at topics for the drill when *you* feel that something has become an issue that is bothering you to the extent that you are feeling emotions of hurt, anger, and the like.

"I would like a drill on the issue of buying a new car," you might say. "Can we set a time for that?"

Under the basic rules, he or she *must agree* to set a time, but your "worthy opponent" is allowed to pick the time and place that is most convenient. If it is your mate who approaches the need to drill an issue, then *you* get to choose the time and place. However, it *must take place within a reasonable time after the request!*

What's reasonable? A week, at the most. Suppose you broach the idea for a ten-minute drill on the car issue on Monday evening after you have had a particularly difficult time starting the old bus that you've been driving for too long. You should expect that by Friday or Saturday you are going to get a drill on the issue.

The use of the ten-minute drill tells both parties that there *is an end* to the discussion of the issue, at least for each ten-minute period. If things are going in a smooth and orderly fashion, feel free to reset the timer for another ten. I have had couples who have worked themselves slowly up to thirty consecutive minutes, all in ten-minute segments, over some fairly hot and difficult issues. The timer's sounding off is a reminder that you have actually engaged in some meaningful dialogue for *ten whole minutes!*

You may think that this ten-minute period will be a piece of cake. Just try it! Ten minutes in a silent room, with no distractions whatsoever, is a long time. You will be amazed at how difficult, awkward, and stilted this will seem at first. But the more you try it, the more it will become a wonderful tool to help you talk *with* each other.

What makes the ten-minute drill such a valuable tool is the built-in escape hatch of the timed segments. You can both walk away from the discussion if it has gotten out of hand, but you must agree to come back to the bargaining table at another time.

Too often couples try to resolve major issues of their daily lives in the midst of all sorts of household confusion. The ten-minute drill eliminates that. It focuses both of you on the specific issue at hand and *forces* you to do some creative listening.

Use the ten-minute drill often as a means of strengthening the new relationship between you and your recovering alcoholic. Make the tool available to both of you on a regular basis until it becomes a natural part of the way you resolve differences of opinion, differences that in the past have turned into major confrontations.

That's the idea of the ten-minute drill, the basic formula, if you will. You use the drill to *prevent* yourselves from burying things so the anger can't be allowed to turn into resentment. If you can safely discuss an issue and reach even a partial resolution of the issue, you have *diffused* it! Doesn't that sound like a better way to strengthen your new relationship? Sure it is!

It wouldn't work in the past, when the old you was busy playing all those seven deadly sin tapes. You weren't able to focus on anything but the alcohol issue. Now, *both* of you can use the ten-minute drill as an exciting way to communicate feelings about any issue that may arise between you. As part of your basic ten-minute drill kit, I suggest you get a bunch of those little magnetic holders that work on refrigerator doors. You use these holders for scraps of papers that you put there. Something comes up in the daily life between the two of you, something that you don't feel right about.

"I would like to drill on that, please," you say. And you write the subject "new car" on a piece of paper. You lock the scrap of paper under the magnetic holder, place it on the fridge door, and it *stays* there until the day of the drill.

More than one couple I have treated had a whole door full of drill items at certain times in their new relationship. But one by one they drilled them out, and soon it was as common to have a special section on the door set aside for drill topics as it was to hang up "A" papers or shopping lists.

One final note: Don't try to hide drill topics from your kids. Explain to them that "these are things Mom and Dad need to discuss." You can be honest with them; there are issues that arise between adults, and this is a new method you are using to discuss them. Your kids will even like the ten-minute drill for resolution of conflicts *they* have with you if they are teenagers or at least over the age of ten.

There are so many exciting possibilities for the two of you to move ahead in your new relationship! I have touched on just a few of the methods that you can use to enrich and better your life together. Notice that all of them, however, involve taking risks. I planned it that way!

You simply must reach out for that brass ring in your life, in your relationship! One of the saddest things that a recovering couple can ever experience is to wonder what *might* have been if they had just taken a risk or two.

As a significant-other person loving an alcoholic, you have gained the insight, through treatment and through aftercare, to know that part of the strength of your relationship from now on will be based on your willingness to express your true feelings about things.

So, go for it! Reach for the brass rings of your life! You might fall off the carousel once or twice, but the great thing is that you have learned how to climb back on and try again. Your new relationship is worth the skinned knees or bruised elbows, isn't it?

20

The Bright Future

We've done it, you and I! You've been taken from A to Z; from anger to two-zooing! Together, we have explored the past, your past, and the terrible imprint that the seven deadly sins made on your life.

You have looked at the present and the manner in which you are now living with the alcoholic you love, hopefully in a state of recovery and sobriety. And now the future looms before you both, a future that can be bright and cheerful and at the same time frightening in its impact on your lives from this point on.

So much is different with you both, and the differences that you are experiencing as a couple become more pronounced with every day of the new sobriety. The grass is greener, the birds sing a more cheery note, the sky appears bluer. All the things that you had wished and dreamed for in a relationship that is free from alcohol may now be unfolding on the panoramas of your life!

All the same, you may have a fear of the future and what might lie in store. That's perfectly natural, and you're entitled to all those "ghosties and goblins" and "things that go bump in the night"! Recovery from alcoholism is a *lifetime* process, and because there is no cure for this disease, you need to be fearful of possible setbacks. But you don't have to be obsessed with possible failure!

How do you stop worrying? Well, one of the things you can do is take a chapter from the fellowship of A.A., which will advise each of you to "carry the message." Essentially, you need to be *excited* about your sobriety, not just *tolerant* of it. You, the significant other, have worked equally hard to achieve the recovering process, and you need to be OK to share that joy with others! How will anyone else know what a life of couple sobriety is like if you don't tell them?

The secret, of course, is obvious. When you pass the message of sobriety for you and your alcoholic, you help yourself stay well. So many recovering couples have a difficult time letting anyone know. What nonsense! Do you *honestly* believe that the people you care about *didn't* know about the alcohol problem? Of course they did! They were just being polite, in many cases at least, and refrained from mentioning the problem and the effects it was having on you and on the relationship that you were enjoying with *them*.

So what's the big deal in sharing the "joy of being sober" with those people who have put up with all the hell that the alcoholism produced? Of course there is fear that a relapse will or might occur. If it does, you address the problem squarely, ask yourself what needs to be done to guard against its happening again, and then pick yourself up and go on with life, full of renewed confidence.

I take great pleasure in telling the significant others that I work with to look at my office door. "Once," I say, "you opened a door and discovered a big grizzly bear standing behind the door! You quickly shut that door, and have been afraid to open *any* door, because there *might* be a bear standing behind *it*, too!"

These were the old tapes of your life that have been playing, the ones that *told* you the bear would be there. What I want you to understand now, having read this book to this point, is that therapy, treatment, and aftercare through A.A., Al-Anon, or other support groups gives you the keys to open any door, without fear!

You can proceed through your life together, knowing that the bear has gone and that, even should he appear briefly, you have the tools at hand to send him scurrying back to his own den. One of those powerful tools is the one that allows you to share with others thoughts and feelings about your new life and how good it can be for them, too.

Sure, you still have to face the stigma of being an alcoholic, co-alcoholic, or co-dependent. Society will talk about the most horrible of diseases and crimes openly, but you may have had the feeling that it's definitely *not* OK to talk about alcoholism. Yet you had no trouble at all surviving the embarrassing situations in the public's eye that the abuse of alcohol caused.

Your humiliation and anger was never so severe that you stopped seeing friends or family, at least for very long periods of time, so what makes it so difficult to talk about the *absence* of alcohol? If you and your recovering person find the word *alcoholic* sticking in your throat, try *recovering* instead!

I still use that term to this day, whenever it seems to be necessary, mostly at parties where (for the 45 minutes or so I stay there) it seems I have to defend my refusal to drink.

"No thanks," I say. "I'm *recovering*."

It never seems necessary to add the word *alcoholic*, since people instinctively know what the phrase "I'm recovering" means. *Never* use the past tense of that word, either! No one, in my opinion, is *ever* a *recovered* alcoholic. Since the process of recovery is a lifelong thing; since the alcoholic is always just one drink away from the next drunk, we must accept the fact that an alcoholic is always in the *recovering* stage, very much in the present tense!

Your use of the tool of disclosure can take great inventiveness, although coming right out and using the "big A" word is still the best! You may want to suggest that your loved one doesn't drink because he or she discovered an allergy to alcohol. That's OK because it's certainly true enough. The alcoholic doesn't handle the chemicals in his or her body the way others do, so claiming an allergy to alcohol is a safe way to state the problem.

Personally, I hope you never use the phrase "on the wagon" to refer to your alcoholic's sobriety. That phrase denotes to me there is the possibility that he or she will

get off the wagon someday, and that's counterproductive
to what your life of sobriety is all about.

There are those who will argue with my even telling
you to talk about the alcoholism of the person afflicted
with the disease. They think it's the alcoholic's place to say
something if he or she wants to. Maybe they're right, but
I don't think so. You have been asked to share even more
of the burden of the tragedy of the disease, and most of it
in public, so what's wrong with allowing you to share the
victory in public?

There is a common courtesy involved, of course. You
will want to make sure that your alcoholic approves of
whom you disclose it to or discuss it with because many of
the persons involved in the life of the alcoholic may not
have really ever known that there was a problem. Job and
other work-related situations are the most ticklish areas of
disclosure. When this situation comes up, I always think
of the wonderful couple that we treated at Gateway a few
years ago. He was a high-level manager in a very responsible position and was very proud of the fact that he had
managed to keep his problem from his immediate supervi-
sor, even though his company had been responsible for
getting him into treatment in the first place.

Upon the night of his graduation from treatment, he
and his wife were in my office to exchange "warm fuzzies"
and to say goodbye to each other.

"The thing I'm most tickled about, next to my sobriety," he said, "is the fact that *no one* from my division
knows I was ever here!"

At that, we shook hands and "George" opened my
office door, ready to go into our meeting room where the
graduation ceremony is held.

"Oh, hello, *boss!*" I heard him say. "George" had run
smack dab into his boss, who was entering treatment
herself and was there for her very first session, which was
attendance at the graduation ceremony! Don't you love it?

The bright future requires you to do emotional check-
ups on yourself. You are still going to have those periods
of time when you will be just plain tired from all the work
that sobriety entails. You will have grown weary at times

from having to go through the "dry drunk syndrome" that your alcoholic passes into periodically. You may have thought you could not dare ask, "Are you possibly having a BUD?" one more time. Yet you have, and you will continue to do so.

But all of these things, these tools of recovery and sobriety, will require a lot of physical as well as mental energy. To help yourself revive, you will need to look at yourself and ask yourself, "What am I doing for *me* these days?"

Have you given up your jazzercise or walking/running program? When was the last time you played bridge with your own special group of friends? What happened to going back to school? In other words, have you put *yourself* on the back burner because you simply have devoted all your energy to your recovering person? Watch that!

For you to enjoy some of the delicious fruits of your victory, you will need to get a little serious again and take good care of yourself. When your own energy level is sapped down to the bare nub, you need to make an emotional check of yourself. Ask yourself:

"Am *I* staying well in every way I can?"

"Have I forgotten *my* circle of friends?"

"Has *my* work been neglected because I've lost sight of my own personal goals for the future?"

If the answer to any of these is yes, then you need to back off and take stock of yourself. There is no way you can meet the new needs of the relationship in recovery if you have not been able to meet your *own* needs. If there is nothing left over to give yourself, then you will soon find that you really are giving *nothing* more to the relationship. You need to guard against "significant other burnout," which is pretty self-explanatory.

So, take stock of yourself and do it often. Get back into the swing of the things that you may have slipped back onto the shelves of your life, fearing that you weren't entitled to anything for yourself. That's nonsense and requires you to give yourself a severe talking to.

In *The Joy of Being Sober*, I introduced the "three Rs of recovery" for the alcoholic to use as a barometer for continuing sobriety. Applied to you as a significant other, they are equally important but need new attention as to how they are defined to meet your specific role in the life of recovery.

The "three Rs of recovery" are:

1. Remember.
2. Reinforce.
3. Renew.

These apply to you a little differently than to the recovering person. For you, it is important that you *remember* not necessarily how it was, but how to *use* the tools that you have at your command when things are at low tide for you.

If you just let the tools lie there on the floor in front of you, or do everything you can to toss them out the window, you risk losing all the things you have gained for your hard work to achieve an alcohol-free relationship. For you, then, the first of the three Rs, *remember*, is to go back over your past. Look at those seven deadly sins of your past and *remember* how they bottled you up and prevented you from taking any action. *Remember* how the old tapes were so easy to play and how the playing of them kept your ears closed to the new ideas that could let you move forward!

Remember the value of risk taking and the importance of going for the brass rings of your life! Without risk taking, you will fall right back into the "pity pot" and perhaps remain there, unable to climb its slippery sides! When you *remember* how making changes in your life has brought you a whole different kind of life, one that is filled with joy and happiness, you will also be willing to *keep* making those changes, on a daily basis if necessary.

The second of the three Rs of recovery is *reinforce*. It is important that you give yourself many hard, stern lectures about how great things have been when you have worked at them. You *reinforce* the behaviors that you know have worked. Every time you put the ten-minute drill to work, it is playing out a message that says, "This can work!" You *reinforce* the ability to settle conflict resolutions between you and your alcoholic in a logical, thought-provoking fashion, instead of in a bloody bedroom battleground! *Reinforce* the use of the "I statements" and how dealing with the way you *feel* about something allows an exchange of thoughts, moods, laughter, and even tears, opinions, and dissensions, on a *feeling* level, instead of on a superficial one.

Reinforce your ability to reach even higher levels of communication by steering those levels away from the inane, gossipy, superficial levels that you operated on for such a long time. *Reinforce* the fact that you have proven to yourself that it is possible to communicate on this kind of deeper, feeling level. Once you have done it, you know that it can be reached, and therefore you must *reinforce* its importance in your life!

Finally, you need to *renew*. This last of the three Rs is particularly important for you as a significant other. You must *renew* your commitment to the relationship that you have worked so hard to get to this point! You *renew* the efforts that it will take from you to keep yourself in a strong and healthy state of mind and body.

Attendance at your own meetings, attention to the details of your own program of recovery, and willingness to *renew* therapy or formal aftercare along with your Al-Anon or adult child work are extremely important. *Renew* the spiritual aspects of your life. If you don't have much of a spiritual life, look into the faith of your childhood or some new one that can provide this vital aspect to your lifetime of sobriety.

Renew your intentions not to let things get buried, as it is so easy for you to slip back into the old patterns and play the old tapes of your past. You will *renew* your desire to stay well and to pass the message of wellness on to those who are still sick.

Finally, *renew* the vow that you will *never again* fall victim to an active alcoholic relationship! *Renew* your intention to do everything within your ability (not *power*) to move yourself into action when action is needed, instead of falling victim to the silken web of the alcoholic spider!

These are the three Rs of recovery for you. Use them! Treat them well and they will not let you down when you need them most.

So, we leave each other full of hope for you and your alcoholic, that special someone who has meant so much to your life that you went through living hell for the one opportunity to *get well together!*

This is not a sad parting, but one that is filled with the hope that somewhere within these pages has been the key to what you have been searching for.

If there has been one small thing, one germ of an idea that has been planted deep within your brain and now germinates to fruition, then these struggles will all have been worthwhile!

If somewhere the painful examination of your past, the hopeful look at your present, and the glimpse at your bright future has caused a glowing spark to ignite deep within you, then you and I will have accomplished a great victory!

Within each significant-other person who has been loving an alcoholic has been a person who has *needed* to be loved. What we have shared together in these pages are miles of a voyage that you must take, one step at a time and one day at a time, to achieve the brass rings that hang so tempting and reachable from the upper arms of the carousels of life.

It's up to you to climb on that carousel and take that ride; no one can do it for you. But if you do, and when you achieve the goals that you have set for yourself—the goals of living a happy, healthy, productive life in collaboration and harmony with your special person—you will truly have realized that loving an alcoholic is a beginning, not an end!

> DE GUICHE: Windmills, remember, if you fight with them . . . may swing round their huge arms and cast you down into the mire. . . .
> CYRANO: Or up—among the stars!

EDMOND ROSTAND, *Cyrano de Bergerac*

Index

ABOUT THE AUTHOR

JACK MUMEY, author of *The Joy of Being Sober* and *Sitting in the Bay Window: A Book for Parents of Young Alcoholics,* is a recovering alcoholic and a professional therapist who counsels alcoholics and their families at his Denver treatment center. He has appeared on dozens of radio and television talk shows, including "Hour Magazine," "Cable News Network," and "Kelly & Company."

BANTAM NEVER SOUNDED SO GOOD
NEW SUBLIMINAL SELF-HELP TAPES
FROM BANTAM AUDIO PUBLISHING
Invest in the powers of your mind.

Years of extensive research and personal experience have proved that it is possible to release powers hidden in the subconscious through the rise of subliminal suggestion. Now the Bantam Audio Self-Help series, produced by Audio Activation, combines sophisticated psychological techniques of behavior modification with subliminal stimulation that will help you get what you want out of life.